Cold Soups,
Warm Salads

COLD SOUPS, WARM SALADS

Irene Rothschild

Illustrations by *Lauren Jarrett*

DUTTON   NEW YORK

DUTTON
Published by the Penguin Group
Penguin Books USA Inc., 375 Hudson Street,
New York, New York, 10014, U.S.A.
Penguin Books Ltd, 27 Wrights Lane,
London W8 5TZ, England
Penguin Books Australia Ltd, Ringwood,
Victoria, Australia
Penguin Books Canada Ltd, 2801 John Street,
Markham, Ontario, Canada L3R 1B4
Penguin Books (N.Z.) Ltd, 182-190 Wairau Road,
Auckland 10, New Zealand

Penguin Books Ltd, Registered Offices:
Harmondsworth, Middlesex, England

First published by Dutton, an imprint of Penguin Books USA Inc.
Published simultaneously in Canada by Fitzhenry and Whiteside, Limited, Toronto.

First printing, June, 1990
10 9 8 7 6 5 4 3 2 1

Copyright © Irene Rothschild, 1990
Illustrations copyright © Lauren Jarrett, 1990
All rights reserved

Library of Congress Cataloging-in-Publication Data
Rothschild, Irene.
  Cold soups, warm salads/Irene Rothschild. — 1st ed.
    p.   cm.
  ISBN 0-525-24889-7
  1. Soups.   2. Salads.   I. Title.
TX757.R8   1990
641.8'13—dc20   89-23773
                                                                          CIP

Printed in the United States of America
Designed by Sheree L. Goodman
Produced by 2M Communications Ltd.

Grateful acknowledgment is made for permission to reprint the following: Green Gazpacho with Salsa Garnish (p. 34), with some minor editorial changes, is going to appear in Mark Miller's book, *Coyote Cafe Foods from the Southwest*, by Ten Speed Press.

To the three men in my life—for their help, support, encouragement, and love—but most of all for their sense of humor!

Contents

Acknowledgments

This book was compiled, tested, edited, and completed because of the help, dedication, and assistance of the following:

First, my agent, Madeleine Morel, who helped make this idea become a reality, and for her patience and encouragement.

Second, my family. My husband, John Rothschild, and two sons, John, Jr., and Robert, whose discriminating palates made them my chief "testees."

My students, without whose responsiveness this could never have been possible, and who consistently prove to me what a worthwhile profession I'm in.

The restaurant owners and chefs who were willing to share their special recipes, and for their cooperation.

Those special colleagues and students, who helped make doubly sure the recipes worked. Frances Barnett, Debbie Hillsley, Sandy Schinfeld, Helyn Spink, and especially Jim Tarantino for his guidance and advice as well.

My friends in the food world for adding their ideas and inspiration. Joel Assouline, Jack Czarnecki, Sonny D'Angelo, Kevin Hill, John Murray, Henry Piotrowsky, and all of the others who helped research products.

Rosemary Altimari and Bernadette Hafner, whose word processor skills helped complete the manuscript on time.

WCAU for giving me the opportunity to meet and greet many other food authorities, and for my audience, whose participation creates constant stimulation.

Finally, John Trapper, my on-air producer, who became my friend and later my assistant, and who helped me through the final stages.

And all of you who are interested in food.

Introduction

As a cooking instructor, caterer, writer, and host of a radio show on cooking and dining, I have spent much of my professional life both teaching cooking and learning, preparing, and talking about food. Over the course of time, styles in both eating and cooking have clearly changed. As a society, we have become aware once again of the real taste of the foods we eat. We are relearning to appreciate the great bounty of this country and to prepare foods that enhance that appreciation. It is no longer considered necessary to cook our food beyond recognition or to disguise it with sauces.

With the availability of locally grown and internationally flown-in ingredients, a key word today is "fresh." We are able to enjoy the crops of the season, and it's a rare cook indeed who doesn't have access to the specialities of other regions. All this helps create new and wonderful taste combinations.

A second key word is "simplicity." A freshly caught, properly cooked fish, a young salad green or vegetable just reaching its peak of flavor, a piece of fruit picked at its ripest—these don't need to be "dressed up." How can one improve on perfection?

The final key to this exciting new cuisine is "quality." The best oils, vinegars, stocks, and seasonings should be used to enhance the natural flavor of food. Some oils have more depth and flavor than others; some vinegars are thin and acidic. Always try to achieve the proper balance of properties—it's the way these ingredients work together that can bring sheer pleasure to the palate.

A few simple rules: use what's in season whenever possible; rely on your own taste buds; and be prepared to sit back and relax with some new taste experiences.

Start with cold soups for brunch, luncheon, dinner, and as a quick and delicious snack. Ingredients may vary according to the season and menu style. Fruit soups are delicious, fresh-tasting, and often marvelous in color. They often have a slight sweetness or tartness, which can be enhanced by the addition of yogurt or sour cream. Vegetables, too, can be cooked and puréed in combinations of vegetable stock, chicken stock, cream, and assorted herbs. In addition to looking and tasting good, cold soups are generally easy to prepare, can be made ahead of time, and are in keeping with the latest trends in healthy eating.

Serving soups as a first course works well, especially preceding a warm salad. I have an aversion to sitting down to a relatively formal meal and being served an ordinary green salad. To my way of thinking, this practice has become tired and mundane. A better alternative would be a cold soup and a warm salad—much more interesting, tasty, and up to date. When you sit down to a warm salad and a cold soup, you can enjoy the wonderful flavors, textures, and freshness—all from foods that are in season—as well as the knowledge that everything is as healthful as it is delicious. And playing on the contrasts in color, shapes, texture, and flavor, plus the interesting taste combinations of hot and cold, makes for marvelous, eye-appealing presentations.

Today's warm salads are unique, although the concept itself is not new. Many foods of this type have traditionally been served in the Orient. "Warm" salads have become very fashionable in France in recent years—particularly those composed of cooked foie gras served atop chilled greens. American tradition contributes such pleasure as Pennsylvania Dutch warm spinach salad, served with hot bacon. This same idea has been used for years in "German-style" warm potato salad.

From California has come a tremendous surge in warm salads, many of them arising under the influence of such well-known, French-trained chefs as Wolfgang Puck, formerly of Ma Maison and presently owner of Spago and Chinois. As the concept of the warm salad traveled east, it was modified and altered according to regional tastes and the creativity of individual chefs. Fashionable in both "trendy" and traditional restaurants, these salads are now moving into the home.

Combinations can be simple—using leftovers or basic salad or vegetable ingredients—or elegant enough to become a first or main course. Popular additions can include duck breasts, foie gras, sweetbreads, or such exotica as jicama, jalapeño peppers, plantains, and even baby bananas. Many of these ingredients become especially tasty when coupled with such products of Asia as Chinese cabbage, bean sprouts, water chestnuts, or lichees. Following some of the suggestions in this book should make it easy to develop your own original recipes—and to develop a whole new cooking style for the 90s.

Stocking the Larder

Keeping in mind the emphasis on "fresh"
- Most of the recipes call for fresh herbs. If fresh herbs are unavailable, dried herbs can be substituted in most instances. Use one-quarter to one-third the amount of fresh herbs called for.
- Fresh lemon juice, lime juice, or orange juice is preferred—but frozen or reconstituted can be substituted.
- I recommend unsalted butter because it's a fresher and better-tasting product. If you must use salted butter, reduce the amount of salt used in the recipe.

- Fresh ground or cracked black or white pepper is a great flavor-enhancer. If you must use pepper that's already ground, do so in small quantities.
- I prefer coarse Kosher salt, which is available in most food markets. Reduce the amount slightly when using regular table salt.

A List of Contributors

A number of award-winning and well-known chefs from the far northwest to the east coast are represented here. They include Jasmine Albuan of The Other Place in Seattle, Washington; Bruce Auden of San Antonio, Texas; Gary Bachman of Odéon in Philadelphia, Pennsylvania; Andrew Berman of Il Nido in Indian Rocks, Florida; Christopher Blobaum of Colette in Los Angeles, California; Donna Ewanciw of Caffé DiLullo in Philadelphia, Pennsylvania; Aliza Green, a restaurant consultant in Melrose Park, Pennsylvania; Pasqulae Ingenito of Windows in Roslyn, Virginia; Hubert Keller of Fleur de Lys in San Francisco, California; Bruce Lim of Ciboulette in Philadelphia, Pennsylvania; Richard Mendoza of The Abbey in Atlanta, Georgia; Mark Miller of Coyote Cafe in Sante Fe, New Mexico; Stephen Pyles of Routh Cafe in Dallas, Texas; Amey Shaw of the Maltese Grill in San Francisco, California; Ronald Shoup of La Fourchette in Wayne, Pennsylvania; Mindy Silver of The Mad Batter in Cape May, New Jersey; Gabino Sotelino of Ambria in Chicago, Illinois; Jean-François Taquet of Taquet in Radnor, Pennsylvania; and Janos Wilder of Janos in Tucson, Arizona.

SOUPS

FRUIT

Curried Apple Soup with Cardamom Apple Sorbet

A good fall soup, both elegant and sophisticated. For tailgate parties, omit the sorbet and add apple brandy to the soup. Or for a warm variation, serve hot with lightly salted whipped cream.

MAKES 8 TO 10 SERVINGS

2 medium onions
4 tablespoons unsalted butter
2 to 2¼ pounds apples
1 tablespoon curry powder
1 teaspoon salt
5½ cups chicken stock
⅛ teaspoon freshly cracked white peppercorns
1 cup heavy cream
Cardamom Apple Sorbet (recipe follows)

Peel the onions, cut in half, and slice thin. Melt the butter in medium-sized saucepan and cook the onions on medium to medium-high heat, stirring occasionally until softened, about 5 minutes.

Cut the apples in half, core, peel, and slice, then add to the saucepan and cook on medium-high heat until limp, about 5 minutes. Stir in the curry powder and salt and continue cooking 1 minute. Add the chicken stock and pepper, bring to a boil, then remove from the heat. Let cool slightly, then purée in a food processor or food mill. Chill in the refrigerator.

When ready to serve, stir in the heavy cream and adjust seasonings. Serve with a small scoop of Cardamom Apple Sorbet

VARIATION: Serve in a mug with a cinnamon stick.

Cardamom Apple Sorbet

MAKES 1 QUART

2¼ cups water
½ cup sugar
¼ teaspoon ground cardamom
1 cup unsweetened apple juice concentrate
1 tablespoon lemon juice

In a small saucepan, bring the water and sugar to a boil over medium heat. Stir until the sugar is dissolved. Remove from the heat and add the cardamom. Cool slightly, then add apple juice and lemon.

Pour into an ice cream freezer and prepare according to the manufacturer's directions. Or freeze in ice cube trays with partitions removed until almost set, then stir. Store in a 1-quart plastic container in the freezer. Soften slightly before serving.

If sorbet is too crystalline, break up and run through a food processor or blender.

Spiced Apricot Lime Soup

This soup is tart and fresh tasting, a nice change from cream-based soups.

MAKES 4 TO 5 SERVINGS

¾ **cup sugar**

¾ **cup water**

¾ **cup dry white wine**

2 **cinnamon sticks**

6 **whole cloves**

2 **pounds fresh apricots, pitted (see Note)**

Juice of 1 orange

Juice of 2 large limes

Lime slices and cloves or cinnamon sticks, for garnish

In a medium-sized saucepan, heat the sugar and water until the sugar is dissolved. Stir in the wine, spices, and apricots and bring to a boil. Reduce to a simmer, cover, and cook until the apricots are tender, about 15 minutes. Let cool slightly, then remove cinnamon sticks and cloves and purée in a food processor or blender. Add the orange and lime juices. Adjust sweetness or tartness to taste. Chill.

Serve either with a lime slice stuck with a clove floating on top, or in a mug with a cinnamon stick.

NOTE: Canned apricots, preferably unsweetened, can be substituted for fresh. Reduce cooking time to 5 minutes.

Blueberry Mint Soup

Having spent many summers at the New Jersey seashore, I learned to use local fresh blueberries and home grown mint in a number of ways.

MAKES 4 TO 6 SERVINGS

3 cups blueberries

2 cups water

¼ cup sugar

6 to 8 sprigs mint or 3 tablespoons dried

Juice of 1 lemon

½ cup dry red wine

½ cup sour cream or yogurt

Sour cream, mint sprigs, and blueberries, for garnish

In a medium saucepan, combine the blueberries, water, sugar, and mint and bring to a boil. Reduce heat and simmer about 20 minutes, until the blueberries are soft. Pour through a sieve, pressing on the pulp. Add the lemon juice, let cool slightly then add the wine. Chill in the refrigerator until ready to serve.

Just before serving, whisk a little of the soup into the sour cream or yogurt. Pour back into the soup, blending it well. Serve garnished with an additional dollop of sour cream with a sprig of mint and a blueberry.

VARIATIONS: A nice alternative to the sour cream and mint sprig is a splash of Grand Marnier and some blueberries floating on top. For a patriotic touch, top the sour cream dollop with a strawberry or raspberry.

Pink Grapefruit, Fig, and Mint Soup

I came across the Il Nido Ristorante in Indian Rocks, Florida, while visiting friends in the Clearwater area. This soup is a typical example of chef Andrew Berman's use of local fresh products.

MAKES 4 TO 6 SERVINGS

12 mission or green figs
Simple Syrup (recipe follows)
7 large pink grapefruit
3 teaspoons sugar
Juice of 1 lime
1 lemon
½ cup chopped fresh mint
12 raspberries

If using green figs, peel them. Poach the figs in the Simple Syrup until tender, about 5 minutes. Let cool and refrigerate.

Squeeze the juice from four of the grapefruits and strain to remove the pulp. Add 2 teaspoons of sugar and half the lime juice to the strained juice. Taste and adjust the lime and sugar as necessary. Chill. Peel and section the three remaining grapefruits and set aside.

Peel the lemon and cut the peel into fine julienne slivers. In a small pan, cover the slivers with water, bring to a boil, and cook over high heat 3 to 5 minutes. Drain and let cool. Squeeze the juice from the lemon and strain to remove the pulp and seeds. Add the remaining teaspoon of sugar and mix well. Combine the peels with the sweetened lemon juice and refrigerate.

Place three figs each in the center of four shallow bowls. Place five grapefruit segments around the figs. Pour the sweetened juices over the fruit and sprinkle the chopped mint on top. Garnish with the julienned lemon peel and three raspberries. Serve at once.

Simple Syrup

MAKES 1½ CUPS

1 cup sugar
1 cup water

In a medium saucepan bring the sugar and water to a boil over medium heat. Cook until the sugar is dissolved and syrup is clear, about 1 minute.

Mango Cream Bisque

Typical of the simplicity and fresh taste of Tucson's four-star Mobil Travel Guide award-winning chef Janos Wilder of Janos Restaurant.

MAKES 4 SERVINGS

3 large ripe mangoes
Juice of 4 limes
1 cup sour cream
1 cup milk
Fresh mint and sour cream, for garnish

Peel the mangoes, cut in half, remove the seeds, and cut into cubes. Add the lime juice and purée in a food processor or blender. Blend in the sour cream and milk, and chill.
Serve in shallow bowls, garnished with additional sour cream and fresh mint.

Melon Ball Soup

This refreshing soup is simple and easy to make. It can be made at the last minute and quick-chilled in the freezer. It's good for a brunch or luncheon as well as for outdoor or summer suppers.

MAKES 4 TO 6 SERVINGS

1 **large ripe honeydew melon (4 to 4½ pounds)**
Juice of 2 limes
2 **tablespoons Midori liqueur**
32 to 36 **melon balls (honeydew and cantaloupe)**
4 to 6 **strawberries**

Remove rind and seeds and cut melon into cubes. Purée in a food processor or blender. Add the lime juice and Midori. Chill until serving time.

Serve in small bowls, punch cups, or cantaloupe halves. Add 6 to 8 melon balls to each and top with a strawberry that has been sliced and fanned out.

Peachy Amaretto Soup

The Amaretto adds a nice almond flavor to the fresh peaches. Serve in a pitcher or in clear wineglasses for a pretty and refreshing summer starter.

MAKES 4 SERVINGS

1⅓ to 1½ **pounds peaches**
⅛ **teaspoon salt**
1 **cup light cream or half-and-half**
¼ **cup Amaretto liqueur**
Plain yogurt, cinnamon stick, or fresh raspberries, for garnish

Peel, halve, remove the pits from, and cube the peaches. Purée in a food processor or blender. Add the salt and stir in the cream and Amaretto. Chill until ready to serve.

Serve with dollop of yogurt, a cinnamon stick, or float raspberries on top.

Orange Cantaloupe Soup with Crème de Mint

This refreshing starter is a creation of chef Amey B. Shaw of the Maltese Grill in San Francisco.

MAKES 6 SERVINGS

6 ripe cantaloupes
1 quart freshly squeezed orange juice
¼ cup Triple Sec or other orange-flavored liqueur
¼ cup freshly squeezed lime juice
Salt
¼ to ⅓ cup chopped mint
6 tablespoons crème fraîche or sour cream

Remove the rind from the melon, scoop out the seeds, and cut into cubes. Purée in a food processor or blender. Stir in the orange juice, Triple Sec, and lime juice. Add salt to taste. Refrigerate 2 hours or until cold. Mix the mint and créme fraîche together. Serve the soup in chilled bowls, garnished with a tablespoon of mint crème fraîche.

Strawberry Rhubarb Soup

A typical taste of Americana, using fresh local fruits in season and California wine. For the Fourth of July, use blueberries for a garnish.

MAKES 4 TO 6 SERVINGS

1½ **pounds rhubarb, trimmed and rinsed**
2 **cups water**
Dash of salt
10 **tablespoons honey**
2 **pints strawberries**
½ **cup red Zinfandel wine**
½ **cup orange juice**
Sour cream, for garnish

Cut the rhubarb into 1-inch pieces. Put in a pot with the water and salt and bring to a boil. Reduce to a simmer and cook, covered, until tender, about 20 minutes. Stir in the honey. Let cool slightly and pour into a food processor or blender.

Rinse the strawberries and remove the hulls. Cut in half and add to the food processor, reserving a few for garnish. Blend until puréed. Remove to a bowl, straining if desired. Stir in the wine and orange juice. Chill until ready to serve. Slice reserved strawberries.

Serve with dollops of sour cream, garnished with strawberry slices.

VARIATION: For a different garnish, use fresh mint or fresh blueberries instead of strawberries.

Winter Plum Soup

This is a good soup to make ahead for that holiday dinner. There's no last-minute fuss or preparation. Serve the soup in punch cups or wineglasses in the living room, or at the table in your best cream soup bowls.

MAKES 8 SERVINGS

1¼ cups water
½ cup sugar
⅛ teaspoon salt
2 cinnamon sticks
1 lemon, peel and juice
Two 16½-ounce cans purple plums
1 tablespoon arrowroot
½ cup red Burgundy wine
½ cup heavy cream
¼ cup Chambord liqueur
1 cup sour cream
Crème fraîche
Ground cinnamon, for garnish (optional)

In a 2-quart saucepan, bring the water, sugar, salt, cinnamon sticks, and 2 strips of lemon peel to a boil. Drain the plums, reserving the syrup. Halve, remove the pits, and purée in a food processor with a small amount of the reserved syrup. Add to the saucepan, reduce heat to a simmer, and cook about 10 minutes. Remove cinnamon sticks and lemon peel.

Blend the arrowroot with the wine and stir into the soup. Cook until clear and slightly thickened. Stir in the lemon juice and remove from the heat. Pour the mixture through a strainer into a bowl and let it cool to room temperature. Add the heavy cream. Blend the Chambord into the sour cream and add a small amount of the soup, whisking until smooth. Return to the bowl, cover, and chill until ready to serve.

Ladle into individual bowls or cups and pipe crème fraîche in concentric circles on each. If desired, run the point of a knife from the center toward the edge of each bowl, then reverse in a symmetrical fashion to create a pattern. Sprinkle with cinnamon, if desired.

VEGETABLE

Black Bean Soup with Guacamole

Serve this hearty and flavorful soup cold with tostadas or corn chips, or hot with a splash of sherry or madeira.

MAKES 6 TO 8 SERVINGS

½ **pound black turtle beans**
1 **cup chicken stock**
3 **cups water**
1 **medium onion, chopped**
1 **celery rib, chopped**
1 **sprig parsley**
1 **small bay leaf**
1 **garlic clove, chopped**
1 **ham bone (optional)**
½ **teaspoon ground cumin**
Salt and freshly ground black pepper to taste
Guacamole (recipe follows)

Cover the black beans with cold water and either soak overnight or bring to a boil, cook 2 minutes, remove from heat, and let sit, covered, 1 hour.

Pour the beans into a colander, drain, and return to a large pot. Add the stock and water and bring to a boil. Add the onion, celery, parsley, bay leaf, garlic, and ham bone, if using. Return to a boil, reduce heat, and simmer, partially covered, 3 to 4 hours until tender. Skim off any fat that rises to the surface. Add the cumin, salt, and pepper. Let cool, then put through a food mill. If preferred, the liquid can be poured off and set aside and the beans puréed in a food processor or blender, then returned to the liquid. Chill until ready to serve.

Serve in soup bowls or mugs topped with a dollop of Guacamole.

Guacamole

MAKES 1 CUP

1 ripe avocado
½ tablespoon chopped onion
½ garlic clove, minced
¼ to ½ teaspoon salt
Freshly ground black pepper to taste
½ teaspoon chili powder
Juice of ½ small lime

Mash or purée avocado in a food processor or blender. Blend in the onion, garlic, salt, pepper, chili powder, and lime juice to desired consistency.

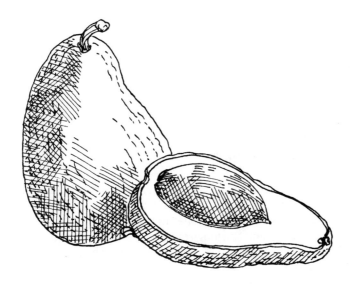

Chilled Artichoke Soup with Lemon

Chef Donna Ewanciw, creator of this wonderful artichoke soup, has been the backbone of Caffé DiLullo in northeast Philadelphia for three years. She and Toto Schiavone, the restaurant director, keep their menu seasonal and simple, always using fresh ingredients.

MAKES 4 SERVINGS

½ cup chopped onion
1 cup chopped celery
2 tablespoons unsalted butter
1 teaspoon minced garlic
1 sprig parsley
3 sprigs thyme
1 small bay leaf
¼ cup dry white wine
Juice of 2 lemons
4 fresh artichokes
3 cups chicken stock
Salt and freshly ground black pepper to taste
¾ cup heavy cream
1 scallion, finely chopped, for garnish

In a saucepan, sauté the onion and celery in butter until softened, about 5 minutes. Add the garlic, parsley, thyme, and bay leaf and cook another minute. Add the white wine and juice of 1 lemon, and cook about 10 minutes to reduce a little. Meanwhile, prepare the artichokes by removing the stems and tough outer leaves, then cut in quarters vertically, discard the fuzzy chokes, and chop coarsely; this should make about 4 cups.

Add the artichokes to the saucepan along with the chicken stock, salt, and pepper. Bring to a simmer, cook for 15 minutes, remove from the heat, and let cool. Purée in a food processor or blender and strain. When ready to serve, add the heavy cream and juice of the second lemon, and adjust seasonings. Serve in chilled bowls, topped with chopped scallion.

Orange Beet Soup with Lime

This is a beautiful pale pink adaptation of the traditional Russian beet borscht. It is a perfect balance of flavors.

MAKES 6 TO 8 SERVINGS

3 bunches beets
1 large onion, peeled
7 to 8 cups water
1 tablespoon salt
3 eggs
1⅓ to 1½ cups sour cream
2 to 4 tablespoons sugar
1⅔ to 2 cups freshly squeezed orange juice
3½ tablespoons freshly squeezed lime juice
Freshly ground black pepper to taste
Orange or lime twist, for garnish

Trim the beets, leaving the tails and ½ inch of the stem end. Peel, rinse, and place into a saucepan with a whole onion. Add the water and 1 tablespoon of salt, bring to a boil, partially cover, and simmer until tender, 30 to 45 minutes depending on size of the beets.

Remove and set aside the beets, reserving the liquid, until the beets are cool enough to handle. Discard the onion. Trim, cut the beets into quarters, and purée in a food processor or blender, adding some of the reserved liquid.

In a large bowl, whisk the eggs with the sour cream and stir in the purée. Return to the saucepan, whisking to blend. Add the sugar, orange juice, and lime juice, tasting for the proper balance. Adjust the salt and pepper. Pour into a bowl or container and chill.

Serve chilled, garnished with an orange or lime twist.

Cold Curried Coconut Carrot Soup

Mindy Silver, executive chef of The Mad Batter Restaurant in charming Cape May, New Jersey, calls this her "Alliteration Soup." The unsweetened coconut milk is available at Asian grocery stores and some health-food stores.

MAKES 8 TO 10 SERVINGS

2 **pounds carrots, peeled and finely chopped**
2 **medium onions, minced**
3 **tablespoons unsalted butter**
2 **teaspoons curry powder**
1 **teaspoon salt**
Pinch of freshly ground white pepper
Pinch of cayenne pepper
8 **cups chicken stock, preferably homemade**
2 **cups unsweetened coconut milk**
1 **cup heavy cream**
Grated carrot or coconut, and chopped parsley, for garnish

In a large saucepan, sauté the carrots and onions in butter until softened. Stir in the curry powder, salt, pepper, and cayenne and blend to combine. Add the chicken stock, bring to a boil, reduce the heat, and allow to simmer about 40 minutes. Let cool slightly, then purée in a food processor or blender. Stir in the coconut milk and heavy cream and chill at least 4 hours.

Serve in chilled bowls, garnished with grated carrot or coconut and chopped parsley.

Curried Corn Soup with Roasted Red Peppers

A perfect way to use corn in or out of season. For a special treat, fold in 1 cup of fresh crabmeat, or top with heavy cream, lightly whipped with cumin.

MAKES 6 SERVINGS

1 **small onion, chopped**
1 **celery rib, chopped**
2 **tablespoons unsalted butter**
1 **teaspoon curry powder**
1 **teaspoon sugar**
1 **teaspoon salt**
Freshly ground white pepper to taste
5 **ears fresh corn or 2½ cups frozen**
2½ **cups chicken stock**
1½ **teaspoons fresh thyme or ½ teaspoon dried**
1 **tablespoon lemon juice**
Dash of Tabasco sauce
2 **cups light cream**
Roasted red pepper, diced or puréed

In a saucepan, sauté onion and celery in butter until translucent. Stir in the curry powder and cook 1 minute longer. Add the sugar, salt, and pepper, while stirring.

If using fresh corn, scrape the kernels from four of the cobs (2 cups) and add to the saucepan, reserving the remaining cobs. Stir in the chicken stock, thyme, and lemon juice, bring to a boil, cover, and let simmer 10 to 15 minutes until the corn is tender. Let cool slightly, then purée in a food processor or blender. Strain, if desired. Add Tabasco, and let cool to room temperature.

In a saucepan or microwave oven, cook the remaining corn. If fresh, remove from the cob when cool enough to handle. When ready to serve, add the corn to the soup along with the light cream, and adjust the seasonings. Top with the diced roasted red pepper or red pepper purée.

Chilled Malanga (Yam) Soup with Fenugreek Essence and Garlic Chives

One of the most creative cooks I know is Bruce Auden of San Antonio, Texas. His use of native ingredients combined with exotic spices creates a most unusual soup. The malanga gives a creamy silky texture to the soup (although yams can be substituted) and should be available in Hispanic markets. Coconut milk is available in Asian markets and some health-food stores.

MAKES 6 TO 8 SERVINGS

½ sweet onion, finely diced

1 leek, white part only, thoroughly rinsed and finely diced

2 tablespoons olive oil

1¼ pounds malanga or yams, peeled and finely diced

½ teaspoon ground cardamom

2 serrano peppers, seeded and finely diced

6 cups chicken stock

1 cup unsweetened coconut milk

Salt and freshly ground black pepper to taste

Snipped chives or garlic chives, for garnish

Fenugreek Essence (recipe follows), for garnish

In a saucepan, cook the onion and leek in oil until tender, about 5 minutes. Add malanga or yams, cardamom, and serrano peppers and cook another minute. Stir in the chicken stock and coconut milk and simmer 20 to 25 minutes. Season with salt and pepper. Chill.

If the soup is too thick, milk or half-and-half can be added before serving. Garnish with chives and Fenugreek Essence.

Fenugreek Essence

1 **tablespoon fenugreek seeds**
⅓ **cup diced sweet potato or yam**
1 **cup chicken stock**
Yogurt to taste

Dry roast the fenugreek seeds in a skillet for 2 minutes. Grind in a spice grinder or with a mortar and pestle. In a small saucepan, combine with potato and chicken stock and cook until soft, 10 to 15 minutes. Let cool, then purée in a food processor or blender. Combine with yogurt to make a mayonnaise-like consistency.

Chilled Roasted Eggplant Soup

During my first trip to Chicago, I had the pleasure of dining at Ambria, along with Giuliano Bugliali and several other food professionals, which was an experience I shall long remember. This soup is an example of the inventiveness of owner Gabino Sotelino.

MAKES 6 TO 8 SERVINGS

1 ¼ **pounds eggplant**
¾ **garlic bulb, separated into cloves**
½ **large onion**
3 **ounces mushrooms**
½ **cup olive oil**
3 **cups chicken stock**
3 **cups heavy cream**
Salt and freshly ground black pepper to taste
2 **ounces prosciutto, julienned**
Fresh basil, chopped

Preheat the oven to 350°F.

Peel the eggplant and cut in half lengthwise. Peel the garlic cloves and the onion, cutting the onion in quarters. Cut the mushrooms in half and put all the vegetables into a roasting pan. Pour olive oil over and roast in the oven until tender and slightly carmelized, 30 to 45 minutes. Cut up the eggplant and place in a large pot with the other roasted vegetables. Add chicken stock and simmer 30 minutes to 1 hour, until all vegetables are very soft. Let cool slightly, purée in a food processor or blender, and strain. Chill.

Reduce the cream by about one-third and let cool. When ready to serve, add cream to the soup. Season to taste and serve with prosciutto and chopped fresh basil.

Potato, Leek, and Fennel Soup

The addition and flavor of fennel is typical of Christopher Blobaum's use of simple everyday ingredients. He now practices his talents as executive chef in the Beverly Pavilion Hotel in Los Angeles.

MAKES 6 SERVINGS

2 medium onions, coarsely chopped

4 large leeks, white parts only, thoroughly rinsed and sliced

2 medium potatoes, peeled and diced

½ pound fennel, sliced, fronds reserved

3 tablespoons unsalted butter or oil

4 cups chicken stock

Salt and freshly ground black pepper to taste

1 cup half-and-half

In a saucepan, sauté the onions, leeks, potatoes, and fennel in butter or oil until softened, 8 to 10 minutes. Add the chicken stock, bring to a boil, reduce heat and simmer 20 minutes. Cool slightly, then purée in a food processor or blender, or put through a food mill. Add salt and pepper. Chill.

When ready to serve, stir in the half-and-half and garnish with the fennel fronds.

Three-Pepper Soup

The contrast in colors and flavors make this easy soup a very special prelude to dinner or outdoor entertaining. It has just a touch of spice!

MAKES 6 SERVINGS

4 large red bell peppers, seeded and chopped
1 large leek, thoroughly rinsed and chopped
1 medium onion, chopped
1 small garlic clove, chopped
1 celery rib, chopped
2 tablespoons unsalted butter
1 teaspoon fresh thyme or ½ teaspoon dried
2½ cups chicken stock
2 cups heavy cream
Salt and freshly ground black pepper to taste
Spicy Green Pepper Purée (recipe follows)

Sauté the vegetables in butter until softened, 10 to 15 minutes. Add the thyme and blend. Stir in chicken stock and cream, and cook on medium heat until reduced by one third. Let cool slightly, then purée in a food processor or blender. Add salt and pepper. Chill.

When ready to serve, ladle the soup into individual bowls and drizzle or pipe Spicy Green Pepper Purée in a Southwest design, or spirals, using a knife to make the design.

Spicy Green Pepper Purée

MAKES 6 SERVINGS

1 large green pepper
1 small jalapeño pepper
2 tablespoons sour cream

    Cut the green pepper in half and lay on aluminum foil skin-side up. Place under broiler 4 to 6 inches from the heat and cook until the skin has charred. Remove and place in plastic bag for 10 to 15 minutes. Peel and remove seeds and stems. Slice the jalapeño in half, removing the seeds and stem, and purée both peppers in a food processor or blender. Add sour cream until consistency of thick cream is obtained.

Vichyssoise Rouge

This vichyssoise takes on a beautiful red color from the beets. The sprouts are a marvelous contrast of flavor, texture, and color.

MAKES 8 SERVINGS

5 medium beets, trimmed

2 cups chicken stock

4 cups water

1¼ to 1½ pounds potatoes (Russet, Maine, or Idaho)

2 leeks, thoroughly rinsed and trimmed

1 celery rib, sliced

1 tablespoon salt plus freshly cracked white pepper to taste

Dash of Tabasco sauce

1 tablespoon lemon juice

1¼ cups light cream

1¼ cups milk

Alfalfa and onion sprouts, for garnish

Trim, peel, quarter, and place the beets in a large saucepan or stock pot. Add the chicken stock and water, bring to a boil, reduce to a simmer, and cover. Peel the potatoes, slice or dice, and add to the pot. Slice the leeks and add with the celery. Add 1 tablespoon salt and continue cooking until the beets and potatoes are soft, 30 to 40 minutes. Let cool slightly and put through a food mill or purée in a food processor or blender. Add the Tabasco and lemon juice. Let cool completely, then add light cream and milk. Season with an additional 2 to 3 teaspoons salt and the pepper. Chill until ready to serve. Garnish with sprouts.

Sorrel Cream Soup

While not a dieter's delight, this is a smooth and slightly tart soup. It makes a beautiful first course and is a true harbinger of spring. It can also be puréed and takes on a lovely pale green color.

MAKES 6 TO 8 SERVINGS

¾ **pound sorrel**

6 **cups chicken stock**

3 **egg yolks**

¼ **cup heavy cream**

Salt and freshly ground white pepper to taste

Cayenne pepper to taste

1 **cup sour cream or yogurt**

2 **scallions, chopped (with part of green) or fresh snipped chives**

Remove and discard the stems from the sorrel. Rinse the leaves well and drain. Bring the chicken stock to a boil. Stack the sorrel leaves and roll up, like a cigar. Slice crosswise in thin strips and add to the stock. Let simmer about 10 minutes. Beat the egg yolks with a fork and stir in the cream. Add slowly to soup, while stirring. Remove from heat and add salt, pepper, and cayenne. If desired, add lemon juice or peel for increased sharpness. Chill until ready to serve.

Whisk some of the soup into the sour cream or yogurt to thin, then pour back into the soup. Serve with additional sour cream, if desired, and top with chopped scallions or chives.

Two-Colored Tomato Bisque with Basil Sorbet Quenelles

Here is a smashing presentation with delicious contrasts in flavors and colors, as used by chef Richard Mendoza of The Mansion Restaurant in Atlanta.

MAKES 6 SERVINGS

7 medium ripe tomatoes
7 medium ripe yellow tomatoes
½ bunch fresh thyme, leaves only
¼ pound shallots, peeled
Salt and freshly ground black pepper to taste
1 pint heavy cream
Basil Sorbet (recipe follows)
6 chive flowers with stems (optional) or 2- to 3-inch lengths of chive tips, uncut

Blanche, peel, seed, and dice the tomatoes, keeping the two colors separate. Place in two saucepans and divide the thyme and shallots, placing half in each. Bring each to a boil and cook on moderate heat until the tomatoes become soft. In a food processor or blender, purée the red tomato mixture. Add the salt and pepper. Repeat with the yellow tomato mixture. Let cool. Add half the cream to each and chill.

To serve, present in large soup plates with red tomato bisque on one side and the yellow tomato bisque on the other side. Using two tablespoons, shape Basil Sorbet into quenelle (oval) shapes and place off center on the red tomato bisque. Lay a chive flower with its stem on a diagonal across so that the flower is on the yellow bisque, the stem on the red.

Basil Sorbet

MAKES 1 PINT

1 cup water
1⅛ cups sugar
¼ cup corn syrup
2 large bunches basil, stems removed and rinsed

In a saucepan, bring water, sugar, and corn syrup to a boil. Remove from heat and let cool. Measure and add 3 parts water to 1 part sugar syrup. Bring this to a boil, add basil, and let steep until cool. Strain, pressing down on the basil leaves, and chill. Prepare the sorbet in an ice cream machine, or place in ice cube trays with partitions removed, in the freezer, stirring occasionally. Store in freezer. If sorbet is crystalline, break up and run through a food processor. Let soften slightly before serving.

Tomato Basil Soup with Pernod

A good blend of summer tomatoes and garden fresh herbs, enhanced by a touch of Pernod.

MAKES 6 TO 8 SERVINGS

1 tablespoon olive oil

1 medium onion, chopped

1 garlic clove, minced

4½ cups chicken stock

3 pounds ripe tomatoes, peeled, seeded, and chopped,
   or 2 34-ounce cans Italian plum tomatoes, drained

1 teaspoon sugar

2 sprigs parsley

1 tablespoon fresh thyme or ½ teaspoon dried

1 bay leaf

3 tablespoons fresh basil leaves or 2 teaspoons dried

Salt and freshly ground black pepper to taste

Tabasco sauce to taste

2 tablespoons Pernod

½ cup sour cream (optional), for garnish

1 tablespoon chopped basil or baby basil sprigs, for garnish

In a large nonaluminum saucepan, heat the oil. Cook the onions until translucent and tender; add garlic and cook 1 minute. Stir in the chicken stock, tomatoes, and sugar and bring to a boil. Place parsley, thyme, bay leaf, and basil leaves in a cheesecloth bag. Add to the saucepan, cover, and simmer 30 minutes. Remove the herbs and add salt, pepper, and Tabasco to taste. Let cool. Transfer to a food processor and blend until almost smooth but still retains a chunky consistency. Chill.

When ready to serve, add Pernod. Garnish with a spoonful of sour cream and chopped basil or basil sprig per serving.

Fresh Tomato Soup with Coriander

Typical of the way fresh ingredients are paired as in this light summer soup, Jean-François Taquet, chef-owner of suburban Philadelphia's Taquet restaurant, continues to receive praise from both patrons and press, and was just honored as one of the Best Chefs of America in 1990 by the Grand Master Chefs.

MAKES 6 SERVINGS

2   **tablespoons olive oil**

3   **pounds ripe tomatoes, seeded and diced, or 2 34-ounce cans Italian plum tomatoes, drained**

1   **shallot, chopped**

1   **garlic clove, chopped**

1   **quart water**

1   **bunch coriander, stems removed**

Salt and freshly ground black pepper to taste

In a saucepan, heat olive oil and sauté the tomatoes, shallot, and garlic for 2 minutes. Cover with water, bring to a boil, and let simmer for 15 minutes. Cool and purée in a food processor or blender along with the coriander. Season with salt and pepper. Chill until serving time.

Green Gazpacho with Salsa Garnish

Another adaptation of the ever popular Spanish gazpacho. This is an inspiration of chef Mark Miller of the Coyote Cafe in Santa Fe, who suggests that it can also be garnished with shrimp or crabmeat as a light lunch entrée.

MAKES 8 SERVINGS

25 to 30 fresh tomatillos, husked and washed

1 medium red onion

2 garlic cloves

1 seedless cucumber (see Note)

2 poblano chiles, roasted, peeled, and seeded (canned can be substituted)

20 sprigs cilantro, leaves only

3 to 4 serrano peppers

Salt to taste

½ cup crème fraîche or sour cream

2 limes, cut in wedges, for garnish

Coarsely chop the tomatillos, saving four unblemished ones for the garnish. Place in a food processor or blender. Chop three-quarters of the onion, the garlic, three-quarters of the cucumber, the poblano chiles, and the cilantro, and add to the processor. Purée, adding ice water to thin if necessary. Add salt, then chill thoroughly.

For the salsa garnish, very finely mince the remaining tomatillos, onion, cucumber, and serranos. Season with salt and chill.

To serve, taste again for salt and add more ice water if too thick. Place in chilled bowls, add a dollop of crème fraîche or sour cream, and a tablespoon or more of the salsa. Garnish with lime wedges.

NOTE: Two regular cucumbers can be substituted. Peel and seed before using.

Golden Gazpacho with Serrano Peppers and Bay Scallops

This golden taste sensation is typical of the originality of Stephen Pyles, the award-winning chef-owner of Dallas's Routh Street Cafe.

MAKES 4 SERVINGS

5 to 6 yellow tomatoes, peeled, seeded, and diced

¼ cup diced yellow bell pepper

⅓ cup diced cantaloupe

⅓ cup diced papaya

⅓ cup diced mango

1 cucumber, seeded and diced

⅓ cup diced chayote

6 scallions, white parts only, diced

3 serrano peppers, stems and seeds removed, diced

¾ cup chicken stock

¼ teaspoon saffron threads

2 tablespoons lime juice

½ teaspoon salt

½ pound bay scallops, lightly poached in aromatic broth and rolled in 1 tablespoon chopped fresh cilantro, for garnish

Combine the diced tomatoes, yellow pepper, cantaloupe, papaya, mango, cucumber, chayote, and scallions in a bowl and set aside.

In a blender, or mini processor, purée the serrano peppers with the chicken stock. Add saffron and let infuse for 10 minutes.

In a food processor or blender, purée half of the reserved tomato mixture. Return to the bowl with the remaining tomato mixture. Strain the chicken stock into the bowl with the tomatoes and stir in the lime juice and salt. Chill soup for at least 1 hour. Divide among four chilled soup bowls and garnish each with ¼ cup of scallops.

SEAFOOD

Coconut Bisque with Hawaiian Prawns

This creative reminiscence of the Hawaiian Islands is the contribution of Pasquale Ingenito, chef of Windows Restaurant and Catering Company in suburban Virginia. A luscious sweet-tasting starter.

MAKES 8 SERVINGS

3 **fresh coconuts**

6 **tablespoons cream of coconut (Coco Lopez)**

1 **pound prawns or shrimp**

2 **tablespoons vegetable oil**

1 **shallot, minced**

2 **quarts heavy cream**

¼ **cup light rum**

15 **white peppercorns**

1 **vanilla bean, split**

Toasted coconut and fresh mint, for garnish

Piercing the two eyes of the coconuts, let the juice drain out and reserve. Crack the shells and remove the meat. Very finely chop or grate and let soak in the cream of coconut and reserved juices while preparing the remaining ingredients.

Remove the shells from prawns or shrimp. Heat the oil and cook the shallot about 45 seconds. Add the shells and cook 1 minute. Add the coconut mixture and the remaining ingredients, except the shrimp and garnishes and bring to a boil. Reduce the heat and let simmer until reduced to two-thirds of original volume. Strain and refrigerate. Poach or sauté prawns or shrimp, cool, and refrigerate.

When ready to serve, add prawns or shrimp to soup and garnish with toasted coconut and fresh mint.

Scallop Bisque with Red Caviar

This attractive and elegant soup works equally well served warm. The red caviar on the chilled bisque gives a touch of glamour as well as taste.

MAKES 6 SERVINGS

4 scallions

6 tablespoons unsalted butter

2 sprigs fresh thyme or ¼ teaspoon dried

4½ tablespoons all-purpose flour

3 cups fish or chicken stock, heated

½ teaspoon Worcestershire sauce

½ teaspoon dry mustard

⅛ teaspoon cayenne pepper

Salt and freshly cracked white pepper to taste

¾ pound bay scallops

¼ cup cognac

1½ cups light or heavy cream

2-ounce jar red caviar

Fresh chives, coarsely chopped, for garnish

Mince the white part of the scallions, including a small part of the green. In a saucepan, melt the butter and sauté the scallions until soft. Stir in the thyme. Remove from the heat and blend in the flour. Return to the heat and cook a few minutes until bubbly. Remove from the heat again and gradually whisk in the warm stock. Blend in Worcestershire sauce, dry mustard, cayenne pepper, white pepper, and salt. Add scallops and poach 2 to 3 minutes, until opaque. Remove from the heat and stir in the cognac and cream. Let cool, then chill until ready to serve.

Serve topped with a dab of red caviar and sprinkled with coarsely chopped chives.

Cucumber and Shrimp Soup with Fresh Mint

This uncooked soup is cool and refreshing at the same time. Chef Jasmine Abuan of The Other Place in Seattle, Washington, adds vegetables, shrimp, and mint to complement the smooth texture.

MAKES 6 SERVINGS

3 large cucumbers, peeled and seeded
½ cup sour cream
1 cup plain yogurt
2 cups chicken stock
½ pound shelled shrimp, cooked and minced
2 tablespoons minced fresh mint leaves
Salt and freshly ground black pepper to taste
Tabasco sauce to taste
Finely diced red onion and yellow bell pepper, mint sprigs, and
    small whole shrimp, for garnish

In a food processor or blender, purée cucumbers and set in a strainer over a bowl to drain, reserving juices. This helps to get rid of any bitterness. Blend the sour cream and yogurt together. Stir in the chicken stock, shrimp, mint, cucumber purée, and use enough reserved cucumber juices to thin, if necessary. Season to taste with salt, pepper, and Tabasco. Chill before serving. Garnish with red onion, yellow pepper, mint sprig, and one or two pieces of shrimp.

Heart-Y Cucumber Soup with Smoked Scallops

This is a special recipe of chef Ronald Shoup, which he serves on the summer menu at La Fourchette in Wayne, Pennsylvania, in conjunction with the Thomas Jefferson University Hospital's Dining with Heart program. Good, and good for you.

MAKES 8 SERVINGS

12 large cucumbers, peeled, seeded, and coarsely chopped
Fresh thyme
2 cups dry white wine
Salt and freshly cracked white pepper to taste
1 pound smoked scallops

In a large saucepan, cook cucumbers 2 to 3 minutes on medium heat. Sprinkle with thyme leaves to taste, then add the white wine. Cook until the cucumbers are transparent. Let cool slightly. Purée in a food processor or blender, then strain. Add salt and pepper. Chill until ready to serve.

Add smoked scallops and garnish with thyme.

SALADS

APPETIZERS

Smoked Bluefish with Two Sauces

What could be easier or more elegant? This makes an unusual beginning to a beguiling meal.

MAKES 4 SERVINGS

Roasted Tomato Vinaigrette (recipe follows)
Horseradish Cream (recipe follows)
1   pound smoked bluefish or sea trout
2   teaspoons chopped fresh dill (optional)
Capers (optional)
**Thinly sliced red onion; lime or lemon slices; black olives;
    yellow cherry tomatoes; fresh parsley; dill or coriander;
    paper-thin cucumber slices; toast triangles or black bread,
    for garnish**

Prepare Roasted Tomato Vinaigrette and set aside. Prepare Horseradish Cream and set aside. When ready to serve, cut the smoked fish into four serving portions. Heat the vinaigrette in a small saucepan, or microwave just to warm. Spread on four warmed appetizer or salad-sized plates. Center each with a slice of smoked fish, top with a dollop of Horseradish Cream, and sprinkle with chopped fresh dill or capers. Garnish as desired with red onion, lemon slices, black olives, yellow cherry tomatoes, or cucumbers. Finish with fresh parsley, dill, or coriander sprigs. Serve with toast triangles or thin slices of black bread. Pass a pepper mill.

Roasted Tomato Vinaigrette

MAKES 1 CUP

¾ pound fresh plum tomatoes
Pinch of sugar (optional)
3 tablespoons extra-virgin olive oil
1 tablespoon balsamic vinegar
1½ teaspoons lemon juice
Salt and freshly ground black pepper to taste
Pinch of ground cumin (optional)
Pinch of ground coriander (optional)

Remove the stem ends from the plum tomatoes or cut in half, if large. Place in a baking dish in a 400°F oven until blistered, about 15 minutes. When cool enough to handle, skin, seed, and juice the tomatoes. Purée the pulp in a food processor or blender. Add a pinch of sugar, if necessary. Blend with vinegar and oil just before serving. Add the lemon juice and salt and pepper. Add cumin and coriander, if desired.

Horseradish Cream

MAKES ½ CUP

¼ cup heavy cream
Pinch of salt
2 to 3 teaspoons prepared horseradish
½ teaspoon lime or lemon juice
Dash of Tabasco sauce

Whip the cream with the salt until soft peaks form. Fold in the horseradish, lime juice, and Tabasco.

Eggplant Appetizer Salad

This salad will hold up to a week in the refrigerator. It can be reheated or served at room temperature.

MAKES 8 TO 10 SERVINGS

2 medium eggplants
Salt
½ to ¾ cup extra-virgin olive oil
1 onion, chopped
1 green bell pepper, seeded and chopped
1 yellow or red bell pepper, seeded and chopped
1 garlic clove, minced
1 teaspoon fresh thyme or ½ teaspoon dried
Salt and freshly ground black pepper to taste
2 to 3 cups fresh tomatoes, peeled, seeded, and chopped, or one 28-ounce can plum tomatoes, drained and crushed
1½ to 2 teaspoons sugar
2 to 3 tablespoons red wine vinegar
1½ tablespoons capers, drained
2 to 3 tablespoons pine nuts, sautéed (optional)
2 to 3 Belgian endive
3 to 4 ounces goat cheese, crumbled
Thinly sliced French bread (optional)

Cut the eggplant into 1-inch cubes. Toss with salt and let drain in a colander for 1 hour. Rinse and pat dry with paper towels.

Heat ¼ cup oil in a large skillet over medium heat, and cook the eggplant, stirring occasionally, until it starts to color. Add more oil as necessary. Remove eggplant with a slotted spoon, then add the onion and peppers to the pan and cook until softened. Stir in the garlic, thyme, salt, and pepper and cook 30 minutes. Add the tomatoes with the sugar and vinegar and simmer until thick. Return the eggplant to the skillet and cook 10 minutes longer. Add the capers and, if desired, the pine nuts. Heat through, about 1 minute, then adjust seasonings.

Rinse the Belgian endive and drain. Remove the leaves and arrange in spoke fashion on appetizer plates or a large platter. Arrange the warm eggplant mixture in the center, overlapping the ends of the endive. Sprinkle with goat cheese. Scoop up the eggplant with endive leaves and/or serve with thin slices of French bread.

Baby Stuffed Eggplants

A delicious up-scale version of the Middle Eastern way of preparing and serving eggplant.

MAKES 6 TO 8 SERVINGS

4 to 5 baby eggplants (1 ½ pounds)
2 to 3 tablespoons extra-virgin olive oil
⅓ cup chopped scallions
2 garlic cloves, minced
¼ pound mushrooms, chopped fine
4 sun-dried tomatoes in oil, diced
¼ teaspoon salt
Freshly cracked black pepper to taste
¼ cup chopped fresh parsley
2 ounces goat or feta cheese, crumbled
Basil Vinaigrette Dressing (recipe follows)

Fill a large pot halfway with water and bring to a boil. Add the eggplants and cook, turning occasionally, until skin softens, about 10 minutes. Remove with tongs and immediately rinse with cold water. When cool enough to handle, slice off the stem end and slice through the cut end to halve lengthwise. Scoop out the flesh, reserving the skins.

Heat 2 tablespoons olive oil in a sauté pan until hot. Add the scallions and garlic and cook 1 minute. Add the mushrooms and cook another minute. Meanwhile, chop the eggplant in a food processor or blender in an on-off motion or by hand until coarsely chopped. Add to the sauté pan and cook until tender, about 5 minutes. Remove from the heat and stir in the sun-dried tomatoes, salt, pepper, parsley, and cheese.

Stuff the mixture back into the skins, mounding it slightly and discarding the extra skins. Place in a lightly greased baking dish and bake in a 350°F oven until heated through, about 10 minutes. Serve at once, drizzled with Basil Vinaigrette Dressing. If desired, spoon additional dressing on the side.

Basil Vinaigrette

1 tablespoon Dijon mustard
2 tablespoons red wine vinegar
1 large shallot, minced
Salt and freshly ground black pepper to taste
.6 tablespoons extra-virgin olive oil
1 tablespoon minced fresh basil

In a small bowl, whisk or blend the mustard, vinegar, shallot, salt, and pepper. Add oil gradually to blend. Stir in fresh basil.

Balsamic Vinaigrette

MAKES ½ CUP

2 tablespoons balsamic vinegar
1 tablespoon red wine vinegar
1 teaspoon honey mustard or Dijon mustard
6 tablespoons extra-virgin olive oil
Salt and freshly cracked black pepper to taste

Blend the vinegars and mustard. Add the oil in a thin stream, while whisking. Season with salt and pepper.

Goat Cheese with Two Tomatoes, Chiffonade

A wonderful new look and taste addition to lettuce and tomatoes. This salad makes a perfect light appetizer, or the quantities can be increased for a luncheon dish and served with some crusty bread or rolls.

MAKES 4 SERVINGS

2 ripe tomatoes

4 to 5 ounces goat cheese

Extra-virgin olive oil

Boston lettuce, romaine, arugula, or combination, and fresh basil leaves

Balsamic Vinaigrette (recipe follows)

5 to 6 sun-dried tomatoes in oil

Fresh basil leaves and sprigs, for garnish

Garlic toast (optional)

Cut the tomatoes into 4 to 5 slices each and lay on a baking sheet lined with lightly greased aluminum foil. Slice the goat cheese to the same thickness as the tomatoes and place a slice on each. Drizzle with oil and run under broiler until the cheese starts to melt, about 3 minutes.

Remove the stems and heavy ribs from the greens. Stack and roll up like a cigar, then slice crosswise into julienne strips. Toss with the Balsamic Vinaigrette and arrange in nests in the center of four salad plates.

With a narrow spatula, slide the tomato slices and goat cheese onto the greens. Slice the sun-dried tomatoes into julienne strips and arrange four strips in a crosshatch pattern on top of each plate. Sprinkle with some chopped fresh basil and garnish with additional fresh basil sprigs. Serve with garlic toast, if desired.

Goat Cheese on Bitter Greens

A wonderful way to begin or end a meal. The crunchy walnuts, tart goat cheese, and bitter greens come together with a walnut oil dressing.

MAKES 4 SERVINGS

8 ounces goat cheese

1 egg

¼ cup light cream

2 to 4 tablespoons all-purpose flour

Salt and freshly cracked white pepper to taste

½ cup ground walnuts

½ cup fresh bread crumbs

Assorted bitter greens (such as curly endive, romaine, arugula, escarole, and dandelion)

2 tablespoons white wine vinegar or champagne vinegar

½ cup walnut oil

Freshly ground black pepper to taste

¼ to ⅓ cup vegetable oil

4 walnut halves, toasted

Cut the goat cheese into four slices or wedges and shape into rounds. Beat the egg and light cream together. In a second bowl, blend the flour, salt, and white pepper. Combine the walnuts and bread crumbs in a third bowl. Dust the cheese rounds lightly with the seasoned flour, dip into the egg mixture and then into the nuts. This can be made ahead, placed on wax paper and chilled.

Wash greens and dry well. Break into bite-sized pieces and put into a salad bowl. The greens can be covered and refrigerated until ready to serve. Blend the vinegar, walnut oil, salt, and black pepper. Set aside.

Heat the vegetable oil in medium-sized skillet. Carefully sauté goat cheese rounds on moderate heat until golden, turning once. Remove with a slotted spatula, letting drain briefly by resting the spatula on a paper towel. Toss the greens with the dressing and divide among four serving plates. Place a warm goat cheese round in center of each and top with a walnut half. Serve at once.

Polenta Cheese Gratin with Mâche and Sautéed Apples

This is the inspiration of Donna Ewanciw, chef of Caffé DiLullo in northeast Philadelphia. When Joseph DiLullo decided to open this up-scale Northern-style Italian restaurant ten years ago, it was the area's first. Now, with DiLullo's Centro, there are two.

MAKES 6 SERVINGS

1½ cups milk

1 cup coarse yellow cornmeal

⅓ cup ricotta cheese

2 ounces gorgonzola cheese

2 egg yolks, lightly beaten

Salt and freshly ground black pepper to taste

1 teaspoon plus 1 tablespoon unsalted butter, softened

2 tablespoons dry bread crumbs

2 apples, preferably McIntosh, peeled, cored, and sliced

1 teaspoon chopped shallots

1 tablespoon honey

1 tablespoon orange juice

1 tablespoon white distilled vinegar

2 tablespoons olive oil

Mâche or other delicate greens

Preheat oven to 375°F.

Bring the milk to a boil and slowly blend in the cornmeal. As it starts to pull away from the sides of pan, remove from the heat and let cool 5 minutes. Fold in the ricotta, gorgonzola, and egg yolks. Season with salt and pepper. Spread 1 teaspoon butter in a 6-inch round baking pan and sprinkle lightly with half the bread crumbs. Spread the polenta evenly in the pan and lightly sprinkle with the remaining bread crumbs. Bake for 15 minutes, until firm. Let stand 3 minutes before unmolding.

While polenta is baking, sauté the apples and shallots in the remaining butter 4 to 5 minutes, until they start to soften. Add the honey, orange juice, and vinegar. Reduce slightly, then stir in olive oil, salt, and pepper.

Have mâche washed and dried and arranged on serving plates. Unmold the polenta and slice into wedges. Put one wedge on each plate and top with warm apples, drizzling the juices over the greens.

ENTRÉES

Fish

Three-Pepper Escabeche on Spinach Spirals

This colorful variation of the popular Southwest escabeche is updated with three kinds of peppers and served warm on chilled greens. Any firm-fleshed white fish can be used.

MAKES 4 TO 6 SERVINGS

2 pounds 1-inch thick halibut steaks or thick fillets
½ cup all-purpose flour
2 teaspoons salt
⅛ teaspoon cayenne pepper
¾ cup extra-virgin olive oil
Fresh spinach leaves, washed and dried
2 medium onions, sliced thin
⅓ cup dry white wine
⅓ cup sherry vinegar
1 bay leaf
2 garlic cloves, minced
1 large red bell pepper, seeded and thinly sliced
1 large yellow bell pepper, seeded and thinly sliced
1 to 2 jalapeño peppers, seeded and thinly sliced

Rinse the fish and pat dry with paper towels. Combine the flour, 1 teaspoon salt, and the cayenne pepper. Dredge the fish, shaking off the excess. Heat ¼ cup olive oil in a sauté pan. When hot, cook the fish on medium-high heat 2 to 3 minutes on each side, until golden brown. Remove and drain on paper towels. Let cool to room temperature.

Arrange 6 to 7 spinach leaves in spiral fashion on each plate and top with skinned and boned (and flaked, if preferred) fish.

In the same sauté pan, heat the remaining olive oil and cook the onions on medium heat until translucent. Add the remaining ingredients and simmer about 5 minutes, until peppers are medium crisp. While still warm, spoon over the fish, drizzling a little over the spinach. Be sure to arrange the peppers and onions in an attractive pattern over top.

Grilled Salmon with Mixed Country Greens and Soy Dressing

This is an example of the lighter style cuisine prepared by chef Christopher Blobaum of Los Angeles's Beverly Pavilion Hotel. Local fresh products are used and ingredients and cooking style are simple.

MAKES 4 SERVINGS

1 **pound salmon fillet**

16 **scallions**

2 **tablespoons minced garlic**

¼ **cup extra-virgin olive oil**

Salt

Freshly cracked white pepper

¾ **pound mixed greens or mesclun (red and green oak leaf, lollo rosso, red romaine, Italian butterleaf, young roquette, chervil, curly cress, or mizuna)**

Soy Dressing (recipe follows)

Heat a grill.

Slice the salmon on an angle into ¼-inch thick medallions. Trim the scallions and blanch for 1 minute. Blend the garlic, oil, salt, and pepper, season the salmon and scallions, place on heated grill, and cook 1 to 2 minutes on each side, being careful not to overcook.

Toss the lettuces with the Soy Dressing and place on a large chilled plate. Arrange the grilled salmon over the greens and the grilled scallions across the top.

Soy Dressing

MAKES 1 CUP

2 **tablespoons lemon juice**

3 **tablespoons soy sauce**

1 **minced shallot**

¾ **cup extra-virgin olive oil**

Blend the lemon juice, soy sauce, and shallot. Gradually add the oil.

Poached Salmon Fillets with Dill Pesto and Wild Rice Salad

This is the ultimate in simple elegance and superb tastes, yet is easy to make with few last-minute preparations. Both the pesto and the rice can be done ahead. The colorful vegetables in the rice are a perfect complement to the salmon, although baby squash—sautéed or steamed and dressed—would work equally as well.

MAKES 4 TO 6 SERVINGS

2 pounds salmon fillets
¼ cup dry white wine
1 large shallot, chopped
1 tablespoon lemon juice
4 white peppercorns
Watercress or mâche
Dill Pesto (see page 60)
Wild Rice Salad (recipe follows)
Cherry tomatoes or sliced fresh tomatoes and dill, for garnish

Cut the salmon fillets into 4 to 6 serving portions, or if very thick, slice on an angle into scallops. In a skillet, bring the white wine, shallot, lemon juice, peppercorns, and enough water to cover the salmon to a boil. Reduce to a simmer, slide the fillets into the skillet, and cook in barely simmering water until flesh is opaque but still slightly pink on the inside. Remove from the heat and leave in skillet while assembling platters.

Arrange the watercress or mâche on one side of each plate. Remove the salmon fillets from the skillet with a slotted spatula and rest the spatula on paper towels a few seconds to drain. Slide the salmon onto the plates, overlapping the greens, and top with a spoonful of Dill Pesto. Arrange Wild Rice Salad on the other side and garnish as desired with cherry tomatoes or sliced tomatoes and dill sprigs.

Wild Rice Salad

1½ cups wild rice
¼ cup extra-virgin olive oil
3 cups chicken stock, heated
Lime Vinaigrette (recipe follows)
1 small yellow squash, diced
½ seedless cucumber, diced
1 small red bell pepper, diced
2 scallions, thinly sliced
2 tablespoons chopped fresh parsley
2 tablespoons chopped fresh dill
½ teaspoon minced fresh rosemary leaves
Salt and freshly ground black pepper to taste

Rinse the rice in a strainer or colander. Put in a bowl with cold water to cover and let sit several hours or overnight. Rinse again and let drain. In a saucepan, heat the olive oil, add the rice, and sauté 3 to 4 minutes. Stir in the heated chicken stock, bring to a boil, reduce heat, cover, and simmer until the rice is tender and the liquid is absorbed, 50 to 60 minutes. Remove to a bowl and toss with some of the dressing. Let cool. Toss with prepared vegetables and enough additional dressing to moisten. Adjust the herbs and seasonings.

Lime Vinaigrette

MAKES 1 CUP

2 tablespoons red wine vinegar or champagne vinegar
2 tablespoons freshly squeezed lime juice
⅔ cup extra-virgin olive oil
Salt and freshly ground black pepper to taste

Blend the vinegar and lime juice. Whisk in the oil and season with salt and pepper.

Dill Pesto

MAKES 1 CUP

2 tablespoons coarsely chopped walnuts

1 small garlic clove

½ teaspoon salt

¼ teaspoon freshly ground black pepper

¼ cup extra-virgin olive oil

2 tablespoons freshly grated Parmesan cheese

½ cup loosely packed parsley leaves

¾ cup fresh dill

½ teaspoon dried basil

Peel and juice of ½ lemon (optional)

2 to 3 sun-dried tomatoes in oil, julienned (optional), for garnish

Blend all the ingredients together in a food processor or blender, adding lemon, if desired. Taste for seasoning. Garnish with julienned sun-dried tomatoes, if desired.

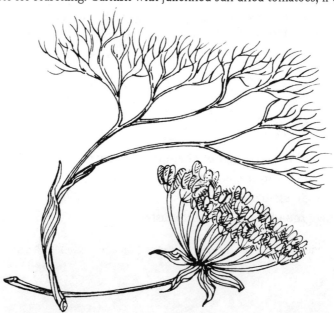

Spiced Squid Salad with Roasted Tomato Salsa

While she started out doing more than her share of cooking chores as chef of several prominent Philadelphia restaurants, Aliza Green is now helping to upgrade other restaurants even more as a food and menu consultant. This recipe reflects her innovative style.

MAKES 6 SERVINGS

4 cups assorted salad greens

2 pounds cleaned fresh squid

1 cup all-purpose flour

2 teaspoons garlic powder

1 teaspoon ground coriander

1 teaspoon ground cumin

2 teaspoons chili powder

1 teaspoon cayenne powder

2 teaspoon dried thyme

1 quart peanut oil

½ cup olive oil

Juice of 2 lemons

Salt and freshly ground black pepper to taste

Roasted Tomato Salsa, for garnish (recipe follows)

Wash and dry the salad greens.

Slice the squid in ¼-inch rings. Rinse and drain well on paper towels. Heat the peanut oil to 365°F.

In a large bowl, mix together the flour, garlic powder, coriander, cumin, chili powder, cayenne, and thyme. Toss the squid in the spiced flour. Shake out into a bowl, using a sieve to strain the squid. Fry the squid in two batches in the oil, then drain well on paper towels. Salt to taste. Toss salad greens with the olive oil, lemon juice, salt, and pepper and arrange on large plates. Top with squid and garnish with salsa.

Roasted Tomato Salsa

MAKES 1½ CUPS

3 ripe tomatoes
1 small jalapeño pepper
½ red onion, peeled
2 tablespoons extra-virgin olive oil
Juice of 1 lime
Salt and freshly ground black pepper to taste

Preheat the oven to 400°F.

Roast the tomatoes, jalapeño pepper, and red onion in the oven about 15 minutes. Let cool. Peel, core, and seed the tomatoes, squeezing out excess juice. Remove the core and seeds from the jalapeño pepper and roughly dice all the vegetables. Dress with olive oil and lime juice, season with salt and pepper, and set aside.

White Beans, Black Beans, and Seared Tuna

Originality and creativity abound in combination with freshly caught tuna, fresh chopped vegetables, and cooked dried beans used by chef-owner Andrew Berman of Il Nido Restaurant in Indian Rocks Beach, Florida, a little oasis tucked away in winter tourist surroundings.

MAKES 4 SERVINGS

8 ounces white beans
4 ounces black beans
½ small seedless cucumber, finely diced
1 red bell pepper, seeded and finely diced
1 yellow bell pepper, seeded and finely diced
1 small red onion, finely chopped
2 ounces chopped fresh cilantro (¾ cup)
4 to 6 tablespoons extra-virgin olive oil
Salt and freshly cracked black pepper to taste
Juice of 1 lemon
Eight slices fresh tuna

Rinse the beans separately and place in two medium-sized saucepans. Cover each with water, bring to a boil, reduce to a simmer, cover, and cook until the beans are tender, but still firm, about 1 hour. Drain and set aside. Combine the cucumber, peppers, onion, and cilantro in a large stainless steel bowl. Add the cooled beans and ¼ cup olive oil, salt, and pepper. Add the lemon juice a little at a time to balance the dressing. Mix gently and refrigerate. Season the tuna with salt and black pepper. Sear in a heavy skillet on both sides leaving the center medium rare. Mound the bean salad on a plate just off the center and lean two slices of tuna against the salad. Drizzle additional olive oil lightly over the tuna and serve at once.

Grilled Swordfish with Orange and Lime Glaze

My good friend from New Orleans, John DeMers, inspired this combination of the fresh taste of the orange and lime with freshly grilled swordfish. A former food editor for United Press International, John's travels and passion for food have led to his most recent book, *Caribbean Cooking*.

MAKES 6 SERVINGS

Red leaf and Boston lettuces

⅓ **cup olive oil**

⅓ **cup orange juice**

2 **tablespoons lime juice**

1 **tablespoon soy sauce**

1 **garlic clove, minced**

½ **tablespoon chopped fresh coriander leaves (optional)**

½ **teaspoon freshly cracked white pepper**

6 **swordfish steaks, ¾- to 1-inch thick**

3 **oranges, peeled and sliced**

2 **small avocados, peeled, sliced, and brushed with citrus juice**

12 to 16 **small black olives**

Orange and Lime Glaze (recipe follows)

Chopped fresh coriander, for garnish

Heat some coals in a grill or preheat the broiler
Wash and dry lettuces. Wrap in paper towels and chill until ready to serve.
For the marinade, combine the olive oil, orange juice, lime juice, soy sauce, garlic, coriander, if using, and pepper. Place fish steaks in the marinade in a single layer. Cover and refrigerate, 1 to 2 hours, turning once. Remove from the marinade and grill on an oiled rack over coals, or under the broiler, 4 to 5 minutes on each side until just firm. Arrange red lettuce leaf on each plate, and put a few torn Boston lettuce leaves off to one side. Place the fish atop the larger part of the red lettuce leaf and arrange the orange slices and avocado slices coming off the lettuce, or as desired. Intersperse a few black olives. Spoon the Orange and Lime Glaze over the fish, drizzling a little onto the lettuce, then sprinkle with additional chopped coriander.

Orange and Lime Glaze

MAKES 6 SERVINGS

1 **cup freshly squeezed orange juice**
2 **tablespoons lime juice**
⅓ **cup dry white wine**
1 **small garlic clove, minced**
½ **teaspoon Dijon mustard**
Grated peel of 1 orange
Peel of 1 orange, julienned and blanched
Peel of 1 lime, julienned and blanched
Salt to taste
White pepper to taste
Cayenne pepper to taste
2 **tablespoons unsalted butter, cut up**
1 **red bell pepper, finely diced**
6 **large pitted black olives, finely diced**

In a saucepan, combine the orange juice, lime juice, wine, garlic, mustard, and grated orange peel. Bring to a boil, reduce the liquid by half, and strain. Return to the pan and add the julienned peels of the orange and lime. Continue cooking to reduce a little further and to glaze the peels. Add the salt, pepper, and cayenne.

When ready to serve, add the butter, bit by bit, shaking the pan or whisking over low heat, taking care to keep it creamy. (Too much heat will cause it to separate.) Add the red pepper and olives and remove from the heat.

Sautéed Tuna Niçoise

The Mediterranean ingredients with the fresh tuna make a delicious light luncheon or summer dish. For variety, the tuna steak can be grilled whole and brushed with olive oil.

MAKES 4 SERVINGS

3 tablespoons red wine vinegar
1 tablespoon lemon juice
½ teaspoon dry mustard
1 garlic clove, halved
½ to 1 teaspoon salt
¼ teaspoon freshly cracked black pepper
½ cup extra-virgin olive oil
5 to 6 medium red-skinned potatoes, cooked
⅓ to ½ pound green beans, blanched
Red or green leaf lettuce
2 ripe tomatoes
½ red onion, sliced thin
¼ to ½ cup Niçoise or Mediterranean black olives
1½ pounds tuna steak, 1-inch thick
2 tablespoons olive oil
1 teaspoon drained capers (optional)
2 tablespoons chopped fresh parsley
Garlic Croutons (recipe follows)

Blend the vinegar, lemon juice, dry mustard, garlic clove, salt, and pepper and let sit 20 minutes. Remove the garlic and whisk in the extra-virgin oil. Set aside.

While the potatoes are still warm, slice, put in a bowl with a portion of the dressing, and let marinate. In separate bowl, put the blanched green beans with some additional dressing. Line a serving platter with the lettuce, leaving a place in the center for the tuna. Arrange the potato slices overlapping in a ring around the center. Place the green beans in spoke fashion or in groups around the potatoes. Slice the tomatoes in half lengthwise and then in thirds. Remove the excess seeds and arrange on the platter. Scatter the onion rings and sprinkle with olives.

Cut the tuna into ½-inch chunks. In a skillet, heat olive oil and sauté tuna 3 to 4 minutes, tossing gently. Place in the center of the prepared platter. If desired, sprinkle with capers. Drizzle the dressing over all and top the tuna with chopped parsley. Serve with Garlic Croutons.

Garlic Croutons

MAKES 10 TO 12

½ loaf French bread (baguette)
Olive oil
Garlic clove, halved

Preheat oven to 325°F.
Slice the bread about ¼-inch thick and place on a baking sheet. Bake in the oven about 10 minutes or until dry. Brush both sides with oil, turn, and rub the tops with the cut side of the garlic. Return to the oven until light golden. These can be made ahead of time and stored up to a week in a tightly sealed container or a plastic bag.

Shellfish

Sautéed Crabmeat with Chile Corn Cakes

A great way to combine juicy fresh crabmeat and fresh sweet summer corn.

MAKES 2 TO 3 SERVINGS

2   tablespoons extra-virgin olive oil
4   medium shallots, chopped
1   small red bell pepper, diced
1   pound lump crabmeat, cleaned
Salt and freshly ground black pepper to taste
Dash of cayenne pepper
3   tablespoons dry sherry
1½   tablespoons drained capers
Juice of ½ lime or lemon (1½ tablespoons)
2   cups fresh spinach leaves, or mixture of spinach and
    radicchio
Vinaigrette Dressing (see page 70)
Chile Corn Cakes (recipe follows)

Heat the oil in a sauté pan, add the shallots and red pepper, and cook until just limp. Add the crabmeat and seasonings. Pour in the sherry and let reduce slightly. Add the capers and the lime or lemon juice and toss over medium heat to warm through.

Wash, dry, and remove the stems from the spinach. When ready to serve, toss with enough vinaigrette dressing to coat. Divide among two to three plates a little to the left of center. Top with the hot crabmeat. Arrange three corn cakes per plate to the right of the salad and serve at once.

Chile Corn Cakes

MAKES 6 TO 9 CAKES

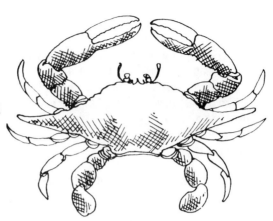

- ⅓ cup all-purpose flour
- ¼ cup white or yellow cornmeal
- ½ teaspoon salt
- ½ teaspoon sugar (optional)
- 1 large egg
- ¼ cup milk
- 4 drops of Tabasco sauce
- 1 tablespoon seeded and diced green chiles (drained, if canned)
- ½ cup corn kernels
- 1 tablespoon unsalted butter, melted

Blend together the dry ingredients. Beat the egg slightly and combine with the milk and Tabasco sauce. Stir into the dry ingredients to blend. Fold in the green chiles, corn kernels, and butter. Let batter sit 20 minutes.

Heat a lightly greased pan to about 375°F. Drop in the batter by small tablespoonfuls and cook until golden brown. Turn until lightly browned on the second side. Remove to a plate and keep covered until ready to serve.

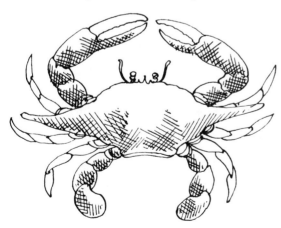

Dandelion Salad with Sautéed Soft-shell Crabs

A perfect spring combination using very few ingredients. You can whip up your own version of Jean-François Taquet's warm salad. Located in Radnor, Pennsylvania, Taquet has been praised by numerous publications; *Philadelphia* magazine's "Best of Philly" issue cited him as best new chef. He has also been selected as a member of the Grand Master Chefs, 1988 and 1989.

MAKES 3 SERVING

6 ounces dandelion leaves or Belgian endive and watercress

2 tablespoons olive oil

6 soft-shell crabs, cleaned

Salt and freshly ground black pepper to taste

1 shallot, chopped

1 large tomato, seeded and diced

1 tablespoon red wine vinegar or sherry vinegar

Vinaigrette Dressing (recipe follows)

Wash the dandelion leaves thoroughly, drain, and layer on paper towels. Roll up, put in a plastic bag, and refrigerate.

Heat the oil in a large sauté pan, add the crabs, and sprinkle with salt and pepper. Cook 3 minutes on each side. With tongs, remove the crabs, add the shallot and tomato, and cook for 30 seconds. Deglaze the pan with vinegar, then remove from heat.

Toss the dandelion leaves with Vinaigrette Dressing and divide among three serving plates. Place a soft-shell crab on each and spoon some of the sauce from the sauté pan on top.

Vinaigrette Dressing

1 tablespoon red wine vinegar

Salt and freshly ground black pepper to taste

¼ cup extra-virgin olive oil

Blend together the vinegar, salt, and pepper. Gradually whisk in the olive oil. (If too strong for your taste, add 1 teaspoon cold water.)

Maryland Crabmeat and Asparagus on Pink Belgian Endive

One of the largest catering establishments in the Washington, D.C., area also boasts a restaurant of equal quality. Chef Pasquale Ingenito of Windows uses pink Belgian endive in this recipe

MAKES 6 SERVINGS

4 pink Belgian endive (see Note)
1 large shallot, minced
6 tablespoons extra-virgin olive oil
2 tablespoons champagne vinegar
Pinch of sugar
32 asparagus tips, blanched
1 pound lump crabmeat, cleaned
1 bunch chives, minced
Salt and freshly cracked white pepper to taste

Rinse endive, remove leaves, and pat dry. Arrange in petal fashion on six serving plates.

In a skillet, cook the shallots in 2 tablespoons of the olive oil about 30 seconds. Add the vinegar, sugar, asparagus tips, and crabmeat just to heat through. Add the chives, reserving enough for garnish, salt, and pepper. Stir in the remaining 4 tablespoons of olive oil and spoon the mixture over the center of the endive. Sprinkle with the reserved chives.

NOTE: If unavailable, substitute white Belgian endive.

Warm Lobster Salad with Fruited Pico de Gallo

The sweet natural taste of the lobster is at its best warm. In combination with the other ingredients, it is almost ethereal.

MAKES 4 SERVINGS

½ bunch watercress

4 scallions, sliced

1½ tablespoons capers, drained

1 navel orange

Orange Vinaigrette (recipe follows)

Fruited Pico de Gallo (recipe follows)

Peeled orange slices, scored cucumber slices, tomato slices, and watercress, for garnish

2 live lobsters, 1¼ pounds each

¼ cup toasted slivered almonds

Salt and freshly ground black pepper to taste

Fresh mint or coriander (optional)

2 ripe avocados

Rinse and dry the watercress, removing the large stems. Place in a bowl with the sliced scallions and capers and set aside.

Peel the orange, removing all of the white pith. Section over a small bowl, reserving the juice.

Prepare the Orange Vinaigrette, Fruited Pico de Gallo, and garnishes.

Plunge the lobsters into a pot with ½ inch of boiling water, cover, and return to a boil. Steam 8 to 10 minutes, until the shells turn red. Remove from the pot and, when cool enough to handle, remove the meat from the tail and claws, reserving the claw meat for garnish. Dice the remaining meat and while still warm, toss with the reserved watercress, scallions, and capers, drained orange segments, almonds, about half of the Pico de Gallo, if desired, and enough Orange Vinaigrette to moisten. Season with salt and pepper and add mint or coriander, if desired.

Cut the avocados in half, remove the pits, and brush the cut surfaces with vinaigrette. Arrange the garnishes on four luncheon plates with an avocado half in the center. If necessary, slice a thin piece off the bottoms to balance. Fill with the warm lobster salad and decorate with the reserved claw meat. Garnish as desired with sliced oranges, cucumbers, tomatoes, watercress, and additional Pico de Gallo, sliced fruit, mint, or coriander.

Orange Vinaigrette

MAKES 1 CUP

1 teaspoon grated orange peel
1 teaspoon Dijon mustard
1 tablespoon lemon juice
1 tablespoon lime juice
3 to 4 tablespoons freshly squeezed orange juice
½ cup extra-virgin olive oil
Salt and freshly cracked white pepper to taste
Chopped fresh mint (optional)

Blend the orange peel and mustard in a small bowl. Stir in the lemon, lime, and orange juice. Gradually whisk in the oil. Add salt, pepper, and mint, if desired.

Fruited Pico de Gallo

MAKES 2½ TO 3 CUPS

⅛ medium honeydew, peeled and diced
½ cucumber peeled, seeded and diced
½ papaya, peeled and diced
1 small tomato, seeded and diced
¼ yellow or red bell pepper, seeded and diced
1 small jalapeño pepper, seeded and minced
1 teaspoon lime juice
1 teaspoon lemon juice
1 tablespoon chopped fresh mint or coriander
3 to 4 tablespoons Orange Vinaigrette
Salt and freshly ground black pepper to taste

Combine all the ingredients, adding enough dressing to moisten and seasoning to taste. Add to the lobster salad and/or serve as a garnish.

Lobster Salad with Green Beans and Salsify

What could be more elegant than warm juicy lobster enhanced by subtle seasonings and cool contrasts? In Philadelphia, Bruce Lim, formerly restaurant chef of The Fountain Room of the Four Seasons Hotel, now takes his talents to his own Provençal-style restaurant, Ciboulette.

MAKES 2 SERVINGS

Radicchio leaves
Spinach leaves
Belgian endive leaves
¼ pound French haricots verts or green beans
Tomato Herb Vinaigrette (recipe follows)
1¼ pound live lobster
½ teaspoon chopped fresh dill
2 to 3 salsify or 2 small leeks
Oil for frying
Curry Sauce (recipe follows)

Rinse, drain, and dry the salad greens with paper towels and set aside. Blanche the haricots verts or green beans in boiling salted water until barely tender, about 7 minutes. Drain in a colander or strainer and rinse immediately in cold water. Let drain, then toss with a small amount of the Tomato Herb Vinaigrette just to coat.

In a large enough pot, bring ½ inch of water to a boil, plunge in the lobster, cover, and cook 8 to 10 minutes. When cool enough to handle, remove the meat from the shell and toss with Tomato Herb Vinaigrette, adding the dill.

Meanwhile, peel the salsify and slice very thin. If using leeks, trim and remove green tops, rinse well, dry, and slice. Heat 2 to 3 tablespoons oil in a small pan and fry salsify or leeks until crisp. Arrange the radicchio, spinach, and Belgian endive on each serving plate. Top with the haricots verts or green beans and lobster chunks. Moisten each with a tablespoon of Curry Sauce and garnish with the fried salsify or leeks. Serve immediately.

Tomato Herb Vinaigrette

MAKES ¾ CUP

1   small shallot, minced
¼ to ½   teaspoon fresh tarragon or pinch of dried
¼ to ½   teaspoon fresh chervil or pinch of dried
¼ to ½   teaspoon fresh chives
Salt and freshly ground black pepper to taste
2   tablespoons sherry vinegar
5   tablespoons olive oil
½   tomato, peeled, seeded, and chopped

Blend together the shallot, herbs, salt, pepper, and vinegar. Gradually whisk in the olive oil, then blend in the tomato. Adjust the seasonings.

Curry Sauce

MAKES ¾ CUP

1   tablespoon chopped onion
1   teaspoon unsalted butter or oil
1   small garlic clove, chopped
1   teaspoon curry powder
½   cup chicken stock
⅓   cup heavy cream
Juice of 1   lemon
Salt and freshly cracked white pepper to taste

Sauté the onion in butter until transparent. Add the garlic, then the curry powder, and cook about 30 seconds. Reduce the chicken stock in a saucepan over high heat to ⅓ cup, then stir in. Add the heavy cream and simmer on low heat 10 to 15 minutes. Strain, then add the lemon juice, salt, and pepper.

Curried Bay Scallops and Green Beans with Tomato-Chive Vinaigrette

San Francisco, which has always been known for its restaurants, can now boast of a renewed interest in classic French cooking with nouvelle overtones. Why not, when its Fleur de Lys, whose chef and co-owner, Hubert Keller, has been dubbed by *Food and Wine* magazine as one of 1988's ten best new chefs.

MAKES 4 SERVINGS

10 ounces green beans, preferably French haricots verts

1 tablespoon olive oil

½ pound bay scallops

Salt and freshly ground black pepper to taste

1 teaspoon curry powder

Tomato-Chive Vinaigrette (recipe follows)

1 head Belgian endive

1 head radicchio

1 head Boston or loose leaf lettuce

Horseradish Croutons (recipe follows)

Trim the beans and blanch in rapidly boiling water 3 to 4 minutes. Drain in a colander and refresh under cold running water. Drain thoroughly.

Heat 1 tablespoon of olive oil in a sauté pan. Season the bay scallops with salt, pepper, and curry powder. Sauté the scallops briefly, add the green beans (warmed up in boiling water) and pour them into a bowl along with the Tomato-Chive Vinaigrette. Toss gently and adjust seasonings.

Arrange the bean and scallop salad attractively in the center of each plate and garnish with endive, radicchio, and lettuce. Decorate with the Horseradish Croutons and serve immediately.

Tomato-Chive Vinaigrette

MAKES ¾ CUP

1 tablespoon sherry or vinegar or red wine vinegar
½ teaspoon Dijon mustard
Salt and freshly ground black pepper to taste
3 tablespoons olive oil
1 garlic clove, minced
1 tablespoon chopped shallot
1 ripe tomato, peeled, seeded, and diced
2 tablespoons finely cut chives
1 tablespoon sliced toasted almonds

Whisk together the vinegar, mustard, salt, and pepper. Gradually whisk in the olive oil. Blend in the garlic, shallot, tomato, chives, and almonds until smooth. Adjust seasonings.

Horseradish Croutons

MAKES 8 CROUTONS

¼ loaf French bread (baguette)
1 to 2 tablespoons olive oil
1 teaspoon drained prepared horseradish
2 tablespoons whipping cream
Salt

Cut the baguette into eight thin slices and brush with olive oil. Toast in a 300°F oven until golden, about 15 minutes, turning once. Add the horseradish and salt to the whipped cream. Spread onto the toasted bread.

Warm Scallop, Potato, and Mâche Salad

Richard Mendoza of The Abbey in Atlanta has a reputation for originality and presentation. This simple artful arrangement with his own special vinaigrette is quick, easy, and appealing.

MAKES 4 SERVINGS

7 bunches mâche
4 small to medium potatoes (about 1 pound)

32 medium sea scallops (about 1½ pounds)
All-purpose flour for coating
Salt and freshly cracked white pepper to taste
1 stick unsalted butter
Vinaigrette Mendoza (recipe follows)
Caviar (optional)

Wash and dry mâche leaves. Arrange in a circle on four serving plates. Peel and slice the potatoes very thin. Over medium-high heat, sauté in ½ stick melted butter until slightly brown but cooked through, about 5 minutes. Remove to paper towels to drain.

Rinse and drain the scallops. Mix the flour with salt and pepper, then dust scallops lightly with flour mixture or seasoned flour and sauté in remaining butter until opaque and just done, about 3 to 4 minutes on moderately high heat.

Overlap potatoes in a circle on mâche. The mâche leaves should still be peeking out from the potatoes. Place the scallops in the center of each plate in a circle, overlapping the potatoes. Drizzle the Vinaigrette Mendoza over all and top with dab of caviar, if desired.

Vinaigrette Mendoza

MAKES 4 SERVINGS

¼ cup fish or chicken stock
2 tablespoons champagne vinegar
½ tablespoon Dijon mustard
Salt and freshly ground black pepper to taste
½ cups grape seed or vegetable oil

Whisk together the stock, vinegar, mustard, salt, and pepper. Gradually add the oil until the mixture is blended.

Scallop and Wild Mushroom Salad on Greens

Succulent juicy scallops, together with woodsy mushrooms and fresh greens, are sparked with tarragon in this salad.

MAKES 4 SERVINGS

1 **large bunch spinach**
2 **bunches arugula or other salad greens**
¾ **pound fresh wild mushrooms (porcini or shiitake) sliced**
1 **pound sea scallops**
¼ **cup tarragon vinegar**
Salt and freshly ground black pepper to taste
1 **tablespoon fresh tarragon or 1 teaspoon dried**
12 to 13 **tablespoons olive oil**
2 **garlic cloves, minced**
Cayenne pepper to taste
Juice of 1 lemon
Fresh tarragon, for garnish

Wash the greens, remove stems and tough stalks, and dry well. Wipe the mushrooms and slice. Set both aside. Rinse the scallops, slice, and drain.

Combine the tarragon vinegar, salt, pepper, and tarragon in a small bowl. Whisk in 9 tablespoons of the oil until blended, then set aside.

Heat 3 tablespoons of the oil in a skillet. Add the garlic and sauté a few seconds. Add the mushrooms and cook until almost tender and juices are almost evaporated, about 5 minutes on medium-high heat. Add the scallops using additional oil, if necessary, and sprinkle with salt, pepper, and cayenne. Add the lemon juice and toss, cooking until just opaque, 3 to 4 minutes. Using a slotted spoon, remove the scallops and mushrooms to a bowl and cover loosely with foil or wax paper. Reduce the liquids in pan by about half and pour into bowl.

Toss the mixed greens with the reserved dressing and put onto individual plates. Spoon the warm mushrooms and scallops on top and garnish with fresh tarragon, if available.

Herb-Garden Salad with "Paradise" Crusted Scallops

This is the masterpiece of Bruce Auden of San Antonio who was named by *Food and Wine* magazine as one of the ten best new chefs in 1988. His interest in natural flavors is teamed with local home-grown products and exotic spices. A natural for home gardeners.

MAKES 4 SERVINGS

2 teaspoons grains of paradise (see Note) or white
   peppercorns, ground

2 teaspoons bread crumbs

2 teaspoons cornmeal

1 teaspoon oat bran

Salt to taste

1 egg

2 tablespoons milk

Mixture of young red and green lettuces

Mixture of fresh herbs (such as lemon basil, salad burnet,
   mint marigold, Italian parsley, chervil, rocket, and
   chives)

16 asparagus spears, trimmed

Red and yellow cherry tomatoes

1 to 1½ ounces crumbled goat cheese

1 to 1½ tablespoons chopped toasted almonds

1 apple pear, diced

16 medium sea scallops

Cornstarch for cooking

1 to 2 tablespoons peanut oil

Bacon Onion Vinaigrette (recipe follows)

Mix the grains of paradise, bread crumbs, cornmeal, oat bran, and salt together. Set aside. Beat the egg and milk with a fork and set aside.

Have the salad greens and herbs washed and dried. Place on four large plates. Leave the basil, salad burnet, and chervil whole, cutting the other herbs into small pieces. Steam asparagus about 5 minutes, rinse in cold water, and arrange it with cherry tomatoes, goat cheese, almonds, and apple pear on top. Rinse and drain the scallops. Lightly coat in cornstarch, shaking to remove the excess. Dip the scallops into the egg mixture, then into the paradise grain mixture to coat completely. In a skillet, sauté in peanut oil 3 to 4 minutes until golden, then place on salads and top with vinaigrette.

NOTE: Grains of paradise is a peppery spice from Africa that can be found in West Indian stores.

Bacon Onion Vinaigrette

MAKES ¾ CUP

- **1 strip bacon, diced**
- **3 tablespoons diced sweet Texas, Vidalia, or Maui onion**
- **2 tablespoons champagne vinegar**
- **2 tablespoons dry white wine**
- **⅓ cup extra-virgin olive oil**

Cook the bacon until it begins to brown. Add the onion and cook a few seconds. Stir in the vinegar and wine, and heat until warm. Blend in the oil and pour over salad to coat.

Warm Shrimp and Artichoke Salad with Orzo

A marvelous combination for all tastes. Blanched broccoli florets can be substituted for the artichokes.

MAKES 3 TO 4 SERVINGS

1⅓ pounds medium shrimp, shelled

One 10-ounce package frozen artichokes, thawed and
    drained

2 tablespoons unsalted butter

Salt and freshly ground black pepper to taste

1 tablespoon cognac or Pernod

1 teaspoon Dijon mustard

2 tablespoons white wine vinegar

¾ cup olive oil

Boston lettuce or blanched kale (see Note)

Orzo Salad (recipe follows)

1 to 2 tablespoons sautéed pine nuts, chopped dill or parsley,
    and fresh mint, for garnish

In a skillet, sauté the shrimp and artichokes in butter until the shrimp turn pink. Season with salt and pepper. With a slotted spoon, scoop out the shrimp and artichokes and drain in colander or strainer. Add the cognac or Pernod to the pan and reduce the juices to 2 tablespoons. Set aside.

Meanwhile, whisk together the mustard and vinegar. Add the oil gradually, blending well. Stir in the reserved pan juices and add salt and pepper. Arrange the lettuce or kale on serving plates and place Orzo Salad on one side in a crescent shape. Portion the shrimp and artichokes next to it and spoon dressing over. Or, make a bed out of the orzo and spoon the shrimp and artichokes in the center. Garnish with sautéed pine nuts, dill or parsley, and fresh mint.

NOTE: Kale—Remove the heavy ribs and stems. Blanch the leaves in boiling water less than a minute to wilt quickly. Refresh immediately with cold water and let drain. They will soften slightly and turn bright green. Dry well.

Orzo Salad

MAKES 3 CUPS

1½ cups orzo
Basil Vinaigrette (recipe follows)
4 scallions, sliced
2 tablespoons capers, drained
2 tablespoons chopped fresh parsley
2 tablespoons chopped fresh dill
¼ to ⅓ cup pine nuts, lightly toasted
1 tablespoon chopped fresh mint

Bring 2 quarts of water to a boil, add the orzo, and cook until just tender, 7 to 8 minutes. Drain, rinsing with cold water. Toss with the Basil Vinaigrette and remaining ingredients including mint, if desired. Taste for seasonings.

Basil Vinaigrette

MAKES 1¼ CUPS

4 to 5 tablespoons red wine vinegar
1½ teaspoons Dijon mustard
1 garlic clove, minced
1½ teaspoons fresh basil or ½ teaspoon dried
1 teaspoon salt
Freshly ground black pepper to taste
1 cup oil (part olive, part corn or vegetable)

Whisk together the vinegar, mustard, garlic, basil, salt, and pepper. Gradually whisk in the oil.

Grilled Sea and Forest Salad

Try an easy, elegant, and eye-appealing barbecue this summer using fresh seafood and local produce. Janos Wilder, chef-owner of Janos restaurant in Tucson, uses fresh nasturtiums in this innovative salad.

MAKES 6 SERVINGS

1 **pound assorted baby lettuces (mesclun)**
½ **cup olive oil**
1 **teaspoon minced garlic**
Salt and freshly ground black pepper to taste
20 **large shrimp, peeled and deveined**
1 **pound tree oyster mushrooms**
1 **pound sea scallops**
1 **pound asparagus, blanched and chilled**
Chili Vinaigrette (recipe follows)
36 **nasturtium flowers**

Prepare the barbecue for grilling, preferably using wood such as mesquite or hickory to enhance the flavor.

Wash and dry the lettuces. Wrap in paper towels and chill. Blend the olive oil, garlic, salt, and pepper, dip in the shrimp, slide onto skewers, and place on the grill. Cook 3 minutes on each side, until cooked but not dry. Toss the tree oyster mushrooms in the seasoned olive oil when the shrimp is half cooked. Grill them about 3 minutes, if they're large enough to skewer, turning constantly, as they cook very quickly, otherwise sauté them in a skillet over grill. Brush the scallops with seasoned olive oil, slide onto skewers, and grill 1½ minutes on each side. Toss the asparagus in the seasoned oil to coat lightly, and also heat on the grill.

Toss the lettuces in enough Chili Vinaigrette to coat the leaves lightly. Arrange on individual plates. Coat the warm mushrooms, shrimp, scallops, and 20 of the nasturtiums in the remaining dressing and arrange on the lettuce. Garnish with the reserved flowers and asparagus.

Chili Vinaigrette

MAKES 1 CUP

1 **egg yolk**
1 **tablespoon chili powder**
1 **teaspoon chopped garlic**
¾ **cup olive oil**
¼ **cup freshly squeezed lime juice**
Salt and freshly ground black pepper to taste

In a small bowl, blend the egg yolk, chili powder, and garlic. Gradually whisk in the olive oil, then the lime juice, salt, and pepper.

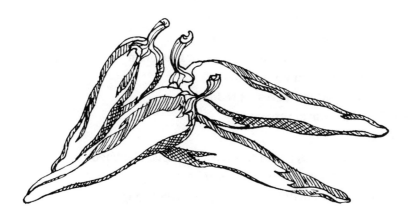

Poultry

Chicken Breasts with Citrus Sauce

The fresh citrus in combination with tender juicy chicken and crunchy hazelnuts will add a touch of class to your menu.

MAKES 4 SERVINGS

1 tablespoon hazelnut or extra-virgin olive oil

4 chicken breast halves, boned and skinned (about 6 ounces each)

¼ cup dry white wine or vermouth

1 navel orange, sectioned, juice reserved

½ pink grapefruit, sectioned, juice reserved

1 tablespoon tarragon vinegar or lemon juice

Fresh snipped chives or tarragon, basil, or marjoram

6 tablespoons unsalted butter, cut-up

8 to 10 red leaf lettuce leaves, shredded

1 head Belgian endive, separated

½ avocado

¼ pound green beans, preferably haricots verts, blanched

Salt and freshly ground white pepper to taste

2 tablespoons unblanched hazelnuts, coarsely chopped

Preheat the oven to 350°F.

Heat the hazelnut or olive oil in a pan and sauté the chicken breasts on medium to medium-high heat until golden, about 5 minutes, turning once. Remove the breasts and place in an ovenproof dish. Roast in the oven until tender, approximately 15 minutes.

Meanwhile, deglaze the sauté pan with the white wine or vermouth, scraping up any chicken bits stuck to the bottom of the pan. Add 3 tablespoons of the reserved orange and grapefruit juices and enough vinegar to make a ¼ cup. If using tarragon, basil, or marjoram, add at this point. Cook on high heat to reduce the liquid to about 1 ¼ tablespoons. Remove from the heat and stir in a piece of butter to blend. Return to low heat and slowly whisk in the remaining butter pieces to finish the sauce.

Divide the lettuce onto the center of four dinner plates. Arrange three endive leaves at the top of each. Peel and slice the avocado, place two avocado slices, overlapping at the upper right, on top of the endive. On the lower right, arrange two sections each of orange and grapefruit, overlapping. On the left side of the plate, place five or six green beans. Slice the chicken lengthwise into four or five strips leaving it connected at the pointed end, then fan out slightly and arrange on top of the lettuce. Add salt and white pepper to the sauce, then strain over the chicken. Add chives, if using, and sprinkle with chopped hazelnuts.

Warm Chile Chicken with Cold Salsa Cruda

This is my own adaptation of a popular dish served at a local restaurant called Carolina's. It is easy and tasty, and the chicken can be stuffed ahead of time. It works well for a crowd.

MAKES 6 SERVINGS

6 chicken breast halves, boned and skinned (about 6 ounces each)

6 small fingers Monterey Jack cheese (about 1 ounce each)

6 whole roasted poblano chiles, fresh or canned

All-purpose flour for coating

Salt and freshly ground black pepper to taste

1 tablespoon unsalted butter

1 tablespoon oil

Green leaf lettuce

Salsa Cruda (recipe follows)

Chopped fresh coriander

Guacamole, for garnish (recipe follows)

Sour cream, for garnish

Preheat the oven to 375°F.

Make a slice in each chicken breast to form a pocket. Stuff the cheese into the chiles and tuck inside the chicken breast pockets. Season the flour with salt and pepper, then lightly dust the chicken, and sear on both sides in the butter and oil 3 to 4 minutes on each side, until golden brown. Place in an ovenproof dish and bake for 10 to 12 minutes. Serve on a lettuce leaf, topped with Salsa Cruda and chopped coriander. Garnish with guacamole and sour cream.

Guacamole

MAKES 2 CUPS

2 ripe avocados
1 to 2 lemons
Salt to taste
Cayenne pepper to taste

Mash the avocados in a bowl or food processor. Add lemon juice to taste and season with salt and cayenne pepper.

Salsa Cruda

MAKES 1½ CUPS

2 ripe tomatoes, peeled, seeded, and chopped
⅓ cup tomato purée
½ small onion, chopped
1 small garlic clove, minced
1 teaspoon extra-virgin olive oil
1 teaspoon lime or lemon juice
1 tablespoon diced green canned chiles
1 small jalapeño or serrano pepper, seeded and minced
¼ teaspoon ground cumin
¼ teaspoon ground coriander
Salt and freshly ground black pepper to taste

Mix together all the ingredients and adjust seasonings. Chill in the refrigerator.

Stir-Fried Chicken with Clementines

The marinade, sauce, and noodles can be prepared ahead and the chicken and vegetables stir-fried at the last minute. Many of the seasonings in this recipe are available in the Asian foods section of the supermarket; otherwise they can be purchased at an Asian grocery.

MAKES 2 TO 3 SERVINGS

MARINADE

1 tablespoon soy sauce

1 tablespoon cornstarch

1 teaspoon chili oil

1 tablespoon dry sherry

1 tablespoon peanut oil

1 pound boneless chicken breasts, skinned and cut into strips

SAUCE

2 tablespoons dry sherry

2 to 4 tablespoons clementine or orange juice

½ teaspoon cornstarch

1 tablespoon soy sauce

1 tablespoon oyster sauce

1 teaspoon sugar

1 cup peanut or corn oil

⅓ cup whole unsalted cashews

1 garlic clove, minced

3 thin slices fresh ginger, peeled and julienned

½ red bell pepper, seeded and julienned

1 clementine, tangelo, or orange, peeled and sectioned

Sesame Noodles (recipe follows)

Chopped fresh coriander, for garnish

Combine the marinade ingredients, add the chicken, and let marinate 30 minutes in the refrigerator. Combine the sauce ingredients and set aside.

In a wok or skillet, heat the oil to 375°F. Cook chicken strips for a few minutes until opaque and they start to stiffen, then pour through a strainer or colander, reserving 2 tablespoons of the oil. Return the oil to the wok or saucepan and reheat. Add the cashews, stir a few times until they are lightly toasted, and remove with a slotted spoon. Sauté the garlic and ginger a few seconds, add the red pepper, then return the chicken and nuts to the wok or skillet. Add the clementine and sauce and heat through. Place in the center of the Sesame Noodles on the individual plates, and garnish with chopped coriander.

Sesame Noodles

MAKES 2 TO 3 SERVINGS

½ **pound Chinese egg noodles, or fresh linguine or angel hair**

3 to 4 **tablespoons sesame oil**

1 **clementine or orange, juice and grated peel**

Dash of chili oil

½ **teaspoon salt**

Freshly ground black pepper to taste

1 to 2 **tablespoons chopped fresh coriander**

Cook the noodles in boiling salted water until just tender, about 3 or 4 minutes. Drain and transfer to a bowl. Add the sesame oil immediately and toss to coat well. Stir in the clementine or orange juice and peel. Add the chili oil, salt, pepper, and coriander and toss. Let cool and arrange on serving plates.

Rumaki in Red Cabbage Nests

This can be a complete meal in itself with its Asian flavors, and vegetables and fruit accompaniments.

MAKES 2 TO 3 SERVINGS

2 slices bacon

2 tablespoons butter

1 pound chicken livers, cleaned and halved

Salt and freshly ground black pepper, to taste

8 water chestnuts, washed and sliced

2 tablespoons soy sauce

1 teaspoon dry mustard

2 tablespoons red wine vinegar

2 tablespoons cognac

¼ teaspoon sugar

1 tablespoon walnut or peanut oil

Red Cabbage Salad (recipe follows)

Alfalfa or radish sprouts (optional)

2 scallions, sliced (with some of green tips)

12 snow peas, stemmed and blanched

1 to 2 mangos, peeled and sliced

In a sauté pan, cook the bacon until crisp, remove, and drain on paper towels. Pour off the excess fat, add the butter to the pan, and heat until melted and it starts to sizzle. Add the chicken livers, salt, and pepper, and cook on moderate heat until tender but still slightly pink, 5 to 7 minutes. Add the water chestnuts to heat through. Remove all the ingredients to a bowl and cover to keep warm. In the same pan, blend together the soy sauce, mustard, vinegar, cognac, sugar, and oil, and warm through.

Arrange the Red Cabbage Salad on a serving plate slightly below center to make a nest. If desired, place a small amount of sprouts around the center depression, then fill with the chicken livers. Coarsely crumble the bacon and sprinkle on top. Spoon on the warm dressing and top with scallions. Arrange the snow peas on the top right edge of the plate and the mango slices on the top left.

Red Cabbage Salad

MAKES 3 TO 4 CUPS

½ **small red cabbage**
¼ **cup white or rice wine vinegar**
2 **tablespoons peanut or vegetable oil**
1½ **tablespoons sugar**
¼ **teaspoon salt**
¼ **teaspoon (scant) hot sesame oil**

Thinly shred the cabbage and place in a bowl. Blend together the remaining ingredients, pour over the cabbage, and toss well.

Tossed Duck Salad with Peaches and Candied Walnuts

This is a "peachy" salad in season. At other times of the year, try preparing it with apples, pears, or raspberries, using raspberry vinegar, or substituting pecans or almonds for the walnuts. This is a wonderful summer luncheon or light supper dish. The rich-tasting duck contrasts beautifully with the cool greens, the fresh peaches, and the sweet crunchy walnuts.

MAKES 6 SERVINGS

2 whole duck breasts, preroasted and cooled (2 to 2½ pounds)
3 large ripe peaches
½ cup walnut oil
¼ cup peach or raspberry vinegar
1½ tablespoons peach schnapps
Salt and freshly ground black pepper to taste
3 to 4 quarts washed and dried mixed salad greens such
    as radicchio, Boston lettuce, arugula, or chicory
1 cup Candied Walnuts (recipe follows)

Remove and discard the skin from the duck breasts and cut the meat into strips. Cut the peaches in half, remove the pits, and slice lengthwise. In a skillet, heat half the oil and sauté the duck and peaches for about 2 minutes. Add the remaining oil, the vinegar, schnapps, salt, and pepper. Stir until heated through and toss with prepared salad greens and Candied Walnuts, reserving a few for garnish.

Candied Walnuts

MAKES 1 CUP

3¼ cups water

1 cup walnut halves

⅓ cup sugar

1 cup vegetable oil

Bring 3 cups of water to a boil and add the walnuts. Cook 1 minute, then pour into a strainer. Rinse with cold water and let drain. In a small saucepan, bring the sugar and ¼ cup water to a boil. Return the nuts to the saucepan and stir well until they are coated with sugar and the liquid is almost evaporated.

In a separate pan, heat the oil to 375°F. Drop in half the sugared nuts and cook several minutes until golden. Remove the nuts with a slotted spoon and drain on paper towels, then spread on greased foil or plate and let cool. Repeat with the remaining nuts.

Store in an airtight container, or freeze up to a month.

Warm Duck Confit with Wild Mushrooms and Seasonal Greens

Odeon restaurant, located in an attractively renovated building in Philadelphia, is one of my favorite bistros. The fare by chef and co-owner, Gary Bachman, is straight-forward and beautifully prepared.

MAKES 4 SERVINGS

4 pieces of confit of duck (see Note)
**5 cups assorted lettuces such as chicory, arugula, and
    watercress**
Tarragon Vinaigrette (recipe follows)
2 cups tree oyster mushrooms

Preheat oven to 450°F.

Place the duck confit, skin-side down, in a small, heavy ovenproof pan or a cast-iron skillet. Roast in the oven for 20 minutes, turning once, until the duck is heated through and the skin is brown and crisp. Do not overcook or the meat will toughen. If necessary, crisp the skin under a hot broiler. Remove the meat and set aside, reserving 3 tablespoons of the duck fat.

Wash and dry the lettuces and break into bite-sized pieces. Toss with only as much Tarragon Vinaigrette as is necessary to coat. Divide the mixture among four large plates.

In a skillet, preferably nonstick, heat the reserved duck fat. When very hot, add the mushrooms and cook over high heat until lightly browned and slightly crisped. Season with salt and pepper and place over the greens.

Place one piece of duck confit in the center of each plate. Drizzle ½ teaspoon of the remaining vinaigrette over each piece and serve immediately.

NOTE: Confit of duck can be purchased through D'Artagnan, Inc., 399–419 St. Paul Avenue, Jersey City, NJ 07306, 201-792-0748.

Tarragon Vinaigrette

MAKES ¾ CUP

3 to 4 tablespoons sherry vinegar
1 small shallot, finely chopped
1 teaspoon chopped fresh tarragon
¼ cup walnut oil
¼ cup peanut oil
Salt and freshly ground black pepper to taste

Whisk together the vinegar, shallot, and tarragon. Gradually add the oils, whisking until smooth. Season with salt and pepper.

Grilled Chicken, Thai Style

Thai flavors are "hot" right now. Increase, omit, or reduce the peppers according to your taste. Thai seasonings are available in Asian grocery stores.

MAKES 4 SERVINGS

4 chicken breast halves, boned and skinned (about 1½ pounds)

1 tablespoon unsalted butter

1 tablespoon palm sugar or light brown sugar

4½ tablespoons Thai fish sauce (Nam Pla)

2 garlic cloves, minced

6 tablespoons freshly squeezed lime juice

2 teaspoons minced and seeded Thai, jalapeño, or serrano peppers

1½ tablespoons chopped fresh coriander

Boston or loose leaf lettuce leaves

Alfalfa sprouts

Flowering red kale, if available, or radicchio or red leaf lettuce

Cherry tomatoes, scored cucumber slices, and scallion flowers, for garnish

Grill the chicken or sauté in butter in a hot skillet, 3 to 4 minutes on each side, until tender. Remove and keep warm in a 200°F oven, or cover with foil. Pour off the excess fat from the pan and add the palm sugar, fish sauce, garlic, lime juice, hot peppers, and coriander. Blend and heat through.

Arrange the lettuce in the center of four serving plates. Place the sprouts on one side and kale on the other side. Artfully place the tomatoes, cucumber slices, and scallion flowers for the garnish. Slice the chicken breasts crosswise on the diagonal leaving it connected at one end. Slide onto the lettuce and spoon the sauce over.

Meats

Buffalo Steak Salad with Yogurt Sauce

Buffalo steak is low in fat, cholesterol, and calories and is usually non-allergenic. By using low-fat yogurt, this is a healthy alternative to beef.

MAKES 4 SERVINGS

2 small garlic cloves, minced
1 teaspoon ground coriander
½ teaspoon ground cumin
Salt
¼ teaspoon freshly cracked black pepper
1½ pounds Buffalo (American bison) sirloin steak
Romaine
1½ cups plain yogurt
2 teaspoons olive oil
White pepper to taste
¼ cup chopped or thinly sliced red onion, for garnish
1 tablespoon fresh dill, for garnish
Pita bread

Blend together 1 clove of garlic, coriander, cumin, ¼ teaspoon salt, and the pepper. Rub on both sides of the steak and let sit at room temperature 30 minutes to 1 hour. Broil or grill 4 to 5 minutes on each side. Do not overcook.

Wash and dry the romaine and break into bite-sized pieces. Place on a platter or on individual serving plates. Slice the steak across the grain into thin slices and overlap on top of the romaine.

Combine the yogurt with the remaining garlic, the oil, salt, and pepper. Spoon over the steak and garnish with chopped or sliced red onion and fresh dill. Serve with pita triangles or halves.

Ground Beef Salad Ole with Plantains

This salad contains a wonderful blend of spicy, sweet, tart, and crunchy, melded together and balanced with Southwest seasonings.

MAKES 4 SERVINGS

Corn oil
1 **medium onion, chopped**
1 **green bell pepper, seeded and chopped**
1 **large garlic clove, minced**
1 **pound ground beef**
One 1-pound can tomatoes, preferably Italian plum style
Ground cinnamon
½ **teaspoon ground cumin**
⅛ **teaspoon ground cloves**
Salt and freshly ground black pepper to taste
2 **tablespoons cider vinegar**
½ **cup raisins, soaked in warm water**
½ **cup slivered almonds**
2 to 4 **ounces grated Cheddar cheese**
Greenleaf lettuce
1 **ripe avocado**
Juice of ½ lime or lemon
1 **ripe tomato, halved and sliced**
1 **plantain or green banana**
Sour cream (optional)
Fresh coriander or parsley sprigs, for garnish
Salsa (optional)

Heat ¼ cup of oil in a large skillet and cook the onion and green pepper until wilted. Add the garlic and cook 1 minute longer. Add the beef and cook, stirring and chopping, until the meat begins to brown. Add the tomatoes along with their liquid and break up using the side of a cooking spoon. Stir in 1 teaspoon cinnamon, the cumin, cloves, salt, pepper, vinegar, and drained raisins, bring to a boil, reduce heat, cover, and simmer 30 minutes. Uncover, add the almonds, and cook until the liquid is evaporated. Keep warm over low heat until ready to serve.

Remove the outer leaves of the lettuce and use two or three to form a cup on each plate. Shred the remainder and mound slightly in the center of lettuce cup. Peel the avocado, slice lengthwise, sprinkle with lime or lemon juice, and place two to three slices alongside the lettuce cup. Arrange two to three slices of tomato next to it.

Meanwhile, peel the plantain and slice on a diagonal, about ½ inch thick. In a small saucepan, heat enough corn or vegetable oil to cover the plantain or banana and fry 3 to 4 minutes until golden brown. Remove with a slotted spoon, drain on paper towels, and sprinkle with cinnamon and salt. Place the plantain or banana on each plate next to the tomatoes. Spoon warm meat mixture on top of the shredded lettuce. If desired, place a spoonful of sour cream in the center and garnish with sprigs of coriander or parsley. Serve with mild or hot salsa, if desired.

Marinated Lamb Salad with Mixed Greens

The Other Place in Seattle, Washington, makes this salad ahead of time in large batches and uses it as needed. It's a great plan-ahead meal for quick-finish casual entertaining. Fresh field greens are used in the salad, the most important of which are mustard greens and mint.

MAKES 4 TO 6 SERVINGS

1 cup unfiltered apple juice

¼ cup kosher salt

¼ cup sugar

1 pound boned lamb, from the leg, trimmed and cut into 6-inch cubes

1 tablespoon olive oil

1 cup Madeira

5 tablespoons Dijon mustard

1 cup dry red wine

1 cup Berango or balsamic vinegar

2 quarts lamb or strong chicken stock

1½ to 2 quarts mixed salad greens, washed, dried, and torn

Combine the apple juice, salt, and sugar to make a brine. Add the lamb chunks and let marinate in the refrigerator 3 days. Remove the lamb from the brine and drain thoroughly.

In a large heavy skillet, heat the olive oil and cook the lamb on high heat until brown and juices have carmelized on the meat. Remove the lamb with a slotted spoon and deglaze the pan with Madeira. Reduce to ¼ cup, stir in the mustard, red wine, and vinegar, and reduce to 1 cup.

In a separate saucepan, bring the stock to a boil and reduce to 1 cup. Combine with the wine reduction and let cool. Cut the lamb into small 1 × ¼-inch strips and add to the reduced liquids. Heat and serve tossed with mixed greens.

Grilled Brochette of Lamb Salad

Aliza Green is one of those natural cooks, whose travels and experience have helped her to evolve into one of the most respected members of the Philadelphia cooking community. She is responsible for developing many of the recipes that are being used in some of the trendier local restaurants, including this lamb salad.

MAKES 6 SERVINGS

2 cups plain yogurt

4 to 6 garlic cloves, peeled

¼ cup fresh mint leaves

¼ cup fresh Italian parsley

¼ cup fresh cilantro leaves

½ medium onion, peeled and halved

½ cup olive oil

Salt and freshly ground black pepper, to taste

Cayenne, to taste

3 pounds boned lamb, from the leg, trimmed and cut into 1-inch cubes

1 seedless cucumber

2 bunches arugula

½ cup extra-virgin olive oil

¼ cup balsamic vinegar

2 red bell peppers

In a food processor or blender, purée the yogurt, garlic, mint, parsley, cilantro, onion, olive oil, salt, pepper, and cayenne. Set aside one-third and place the remainder in a stainless steel or glass bowl. Add the lamb, cover, and refrigerate overnight.

When ready to serve, light the grill (preferably hardwood charcoal) or preheat the broiler. Slice the cucumber into ¼-inch slices and dress with the reserved marinade. Wash and dry the arugula, then dress with the extra-virgin olive oil, balsamic vinegar, salt, and pepper. Roast, peel, and seed the peppers; cut into strips. Thread the lamb onto skewers and grill 8 to 10 minutes, turning once. Place the arugula in the center of a plate and top with the lamb brochette. Arrange the cucumbers and the roasted peppers on either side.

Composed Veal Salad

This makes a very elegant entrée for that special occasion.

MAKES 4 SERVINGS

¼ cup all-purpose flour

¼ teaspoon salt

4 grinds white pepper

1 to 1¼ pounds veal scallops, cut from leg or rump

5 to 6 tablespoons unsalted butter

2½ tablespoons olive oil

½ cup dry white wine

1 tablespoon fresh tarragon or ½ teaspoon dried

½ teaspoon Dijon mustard

1½ teaspoons balsamic vinegar

Salt and freshly ground black pepper to taste

4 cups washed and dried salad greens (4 to 5 leaves
     radicchio, torn in half; 6 stems arugula; 4 to 5 leaves
     mâche; and bibb or Boston lettuce

2 ripe tomatoes, thinly sliced

2 large canned artichoke hearts, drained and halved

1 ripe avocado, peeled and quartered

Niçoise olives (optional), for garnish

Combine the flour, salt, and pepper on a large plate. Using a flat mallet or rolling pin, pound the veal to ⅛- to ¼-inch thickness. Heat 2 tablespoons butter with 1 tablespoon oil in a large skillet until sizzling. Dredge the veal in the seasoned flour, shaking to remove excess, then sauté in batches until lightly browned, 1 to 1½ minutes per side. Remove to a plate, cover loosely with aluminum foil, and keep warm. Add the wine and tarragon to the skillet and reduce a little, scraping up the drippings with a wooden spoon. Turn off the heat and whisk in the remaining butter, tablespoon by tablespoon, just before serving.

Combine the mustard, vinegar, salt, and pepper to make the dressing. Gradually drizzle in the remaining 1½ tablespoons of olive oil, while whisking. Toss the salad greens with the dressing just before serving.

Arrange the sliced tomato along one side of each plate and place a fanned artichoke heart at one end and a fanned avocado quarter at the opposite end. Place the tossed salad greens down the center of each plate, arrange the veal scallops, overlapping, on the opposite side of the plate, the spoon the warm veal sauce over and serve immediately.

Steak and Caesar Salad

This is a hearty tasty combination of Caesar salad and steak all in one. Any tender cut of beef, or leftover pieces of filet, can be used.

MAKES 6 TO 8 SERVINGS

2 heads romaine
1 egg
½ cup vegetable oil
¼ cup olive oil
3 tablespoons freshly squeezed lemon juice
1½ to 2 tablespoons red wine vinegar
½ teaspoon dry mustard
½ teaspoon Worcestershire sauce
1 large garlic glove, minced
Salt and freshly cracked black pepper to taste
½ cup freshly grated Parmesan cheese
¼ to ⅓ cup crumbled blue cheese
1 cup croutons (optional)
1½ pounds strip, sirloin, flank, or filet beefsteak pieces,
trimmed, ¾- to 1-inch thick

Wash the romaine leaves, dry well, and tear into bite-sized pieces. Wrap in layers of paper towels, put in plastic bag, and refrigerate to keep crisp. Combine the oils, lemon juice, vinegar, mustard, Worcestershire, garlic, about 1 teaspoon of salt, and ¼ teaspoon pepper, whisking well to blend. Set aside.

When ready to serve, bring the steak to room temperature. Place the romaine in a large salad bowl and add the Parmesan cheese, blue cheese, and croutons, if using. Cook the steak on a hot grill, or pan-fry in a heavy skillet over high heat for approximately 4 to 5 minutes on each side, for medium-rare. Sprinkle with salt and pepper after turning once. Slice the steak across the grain in thin slices and add to the salad. Pour on dressing and any meat juices, toss, and serve immediately.

Pass extra Parmesan cheese and a pepper mill.

Lamb Melba

The delicate flavors of the peaches and red raspberries served with the rack of lamb are especially appealing for a Valentine menu or a dinner for two.

MAKES 3 TO 4 SERVINGS

½ rack of lamb (2 to 3 pounds)

1 to 2 tablespoons unsalted butter

All-purpose flour for coating

⅛ teaspoon salt

4 tablespoons cognac

6 tablespoons heavy cream

¾ cup peeled sliced peaches, fresh or canned

4½ tablespoons each peach or raspberry vinegar

⅛ teaspoon salt

2 teaspoons fresh tarragon or 1 teaspoon dried

Large head radicchio

Boston or bibb lettuce

Watercress

2 tablespoons fresh raspberries

2 tablespoons sliced toasted almonds

Trim the meat from the bones and cut into 8 slices. Heat the butter in a sauté pan and dredge the meat lightly in flour and salt, shaking off the excess. Sauté 1½ to 2 minutes on each side until the lamb is lightly browned but still sightly pink on the inside. Remove from the pan, cover with aluminum foil, and keep warm. Pour off the excess fat from the pan and remove from the heat. Add 1½ tablespoons cognac and flambé, scraping up the drippings with a wooden spoon. Return to the heat, add the cream, and reduce over high heat until thickened. Add the peaches (if using canned, add 2 tablespoons syrup), vinegar, and the remaining cognac, and cook until the peaches are tender. Stir in salt, pepper, and tarragon.

Arrange a large radicchio leaf on each plate. Top with two lettuce leaves and place a small bouquet of watercress in the center. Arrange 2 to 3 lamb medallions overlapping on one side and peaches on the other. Sprinkle the greens with raspberries and almonds. Drizzle the sauce over meat and greens and serve at once.

Sweetbreads on Exotic Greens with Blueberry Beurre Blanc

This nouvelle-style recipe from La Fourchette in Wayne, Pennsylvania, reflects the inventiveness of chef Ronald Shoup. He was recently named as one of the 1989 "Chefs of America" by the Grand Master Chefs.

MAKES 4 SERVINGS

4 to 5½ ounces arugula and mixed greens such as garden cress or watercress, dandelion greens, chickweed, garlic mustard, chicory, or soft-leaf lettuce

12 ounces sweetbreads

Dry white wine

Splash of white wine vinegar

Salt and freshly cracked white pepper to taste

¼ cup dry white wine

1 tablespoon blueberry vinegar

1 small shallot, minced

½ cup fresh blueberries

¼ pound plus 2 tablespoons unsalted butter

Blueberries, for garnish

Wash and dry all the greens and set aside.

In a small saucepan, cook the sweetbreads in water to cover, along with a splash of white wine, the white wine vinegar, salt, and white pepper. Simmer 20 to 25 minutes until just tender, remove from the liquid, and, when cool enough to handle, remove the skin and veins.

In a separate small saucepan, heat ¼ cup white wine, the blueberry vinegar, shallot, and blueberries. Cook on high heat until liquids are almost evaporated. Set aside.

Meanwhile, divide the greens onto four serving plates. When ready to serve, sauté the sweetbreads in additional butter until golden brown, slice, and place atop the greens. To finish the sauce, rewarm, if necessary, and add the butter bit by bit, whisking or shaking the pan until sauce is creamy, taking care not to let the sauce separate. Strain through a fine sieve and season with salt and pepper. Spoon over the sweetbreads, and drizzle over the greens. Garnish with additional blueberries.

SIDE DISHES

Asparagus with Roasted Red Pepper Vinaigrette

This salad, which has an interesting delicious flavor and color contrast, makes a smashing vegetable course.

MAKES 6 SERVINGS

1 pound medium fresh asparagus
Salt to taste
2 tablespoons butter, melted
Freshly squeezed lemon juice
Red Pepper Vinaigrette (recipe follows)
1 tablespoon snipped chives

Break the butt ends off the asparagus and peel the stalks. Bring a shallow pan of water to a boil, add the salt and asparagus, and cook until tender, 5 to 7 minutes. Remove to paper towels to drain and place immediately onto serving plates. Combine butter and a few drops of lemon juice and brush the asparagus with the melted butter and lemon juice, spooning the Red Pepper Vinaigrette over the centers. Sprinkle with snipped chives and serve at once.

Red Pepper Vinaigrette

MAKES 1 CUP

1 **large red bell pepper**
2 **tablespoons plus ⅓ cup olive oil**
1½ **tablespoons red wine vinegar**
1 **teaspoon Dijon mustard**
1 **large shallot, finely chopped**
¼ **teaspoon salt**
Freshly cracked pepper to taste

Roast the pepper on a long fork directly over a gas flame, rotating until it is charred all over. Or, cut in half and place under the broiler, skin-side up, until blackened. Remove to a plastic bag and let steam until cool enough to handle. Peel the skins and discard. Remove the stem, seeds, and ribs. Cut into a large dice and purée in a food processor or blender with 2 tablespoons of oil until smooth.

In a small bowl or measuring cup, blend the vinegar, mustard, shallot, salt, and pepper. Slowly whisk in the remaining ⅓ cup oil. Add the red pepper purée and adjust seasonings.

Asparagus with Maple Vinaigrette and Roasted Pecans

This wonderful spring salad, using asparagus in season, is the creation of chef Mindy Silver of The Mad Batter Restaurant in Cape May, New Jersey. Her dressing contains maple syrup, and the salad is topped with roasted pecans.

MAKES 4 TO 6 SERVINGS

1 pound medium fresh asparagus

Assorted greens (red-leaf lettuce, green leaf lettuce, Boston, bibb), washed and dried

Pinch of freshly cracked white pepper

Maple Vinaigrette (recipe follows)

½ cup roasted pecans

Break the butt ends off the asparagus and peel the stalks. Bring a shallow pan of water to a boil, add the salt and asparagus, and cook until tender, 5 to 7 minutes. Arrange the greens on serving plates. Group the warm asparagus in the center of each plate and spoon the Maple Vinaigrette over. Sprinkle with pecans and serve immediately.

Maple Vinaigrette

MAKES 1 CUP

3 tablespoons sherry vinegar or raspberry vinegar

2 teaspoons Dijon mustard

1 garlic clove, minced

¼ teaspoon salt

Pinch of freshly cracked white pepper

¾ cup vegetable oil

3 tablespoons maple syrup

1½ teaspoons chopped fresh tarragon or ¾ teaspoon dried

Combine the vinegar, mustard, garlic, salt, and pepper and blend well. Gradually whisk in the oil, then the maple syrup and tarragon.

Wilted Southern Greens with Apples, Pecans, and Cranberries

An inventive use of American salad ingredients as presented by Dallas's Routh Street Cafe chef, Stephen Pyles.

MAKES 4 SERVINGS

½ pound assorted greens such as turnips, collards, and
  mustards
¾ cup fresh cranberries
¼ cup sugar
¼ pound bacon, diced
2 shallots, minced
2 garlic cloves, minced
½ cup corn oil
⅛ cup balsamic vinegar
⅛ cup red wine vinegar
2 sprigs rosemary, chopped
½ cup chopped toasted pecans
2 green apples, cored and coarsely chopped
Salt and freshly ground black pepper to taste

Wash and dry the assorted greens and set aside. Chop the cranberries coarsely and macerate in the sugar until ready to use.

In a large skillet, cook the bacon until crisp, then remove with a slotted spoon, leaving the fat in pan, and drain on paper towels. Add the shallot and garlic and cook until soft. Whisk in the oil and vinegars, add the rosemary, pecans, apples, and cranberries and cook for 1 minute. Add the greens and toss for 10 seconds. Season with salt and pepper and divide among four plates. Sprinkle reserved bacon on top.

Four-Endive Salad with Hot Pancetta Dressing

Delicious variation of a wilted greens salad using four varieties of endive (chicory, escarole, radicchio, and Belgian) and touches of Italia.

MAKES 8 SERVINGS

½ head curly endive (chicory)

½ head escarole

1 small head radicchio

1 Belgian endive

½ large red onion, sliced

¼ cup freshly grated Parmesan cheese (optional)

Six ¼-inch slices of pancetta or slab bacon (about ¾ pound)

¼ cup balsamic vinegar

½ teaspoon dry mustard

2 tablespoons sugar

⅓ cup extra-virgin olive oil

2 egg yolks, lightly beaten

1 tablespoon fresh rosemary leaves

1 tablespoon chopped fresh parsley

½ teaspoon salt

Freshly cracked black pepper to taste

Remove the root ends and tough stalks from the curly endive and escarole. Remove the leaves from the radicchio and peel the leaves from Belgian endive. Rinse and drain well. Tear into bite-sized pieces and place on paper towels. When ready to serve, toss the curly endive, escarole, radicchio, Belgian endive, red onion, and Parmesan cheese, if using, in a salad bowl.

Dice the pancetta or bacon in ¼-inch pieces and cook in a small skillet until crisp, remove with a slotted spoon and drain on paper towels, then add to salad ingredients, reserving drippings. Remove the skillet from the heat and immediately whisk in the vinegar, mustard, sugar, and olive oil. Gradually whisk in beaten egg yolks. Add the rosemary, parsley, salt, and pepper. Pour over the salad ingredients and serve at once.

Fresh Herb and Wild Mushroom Salad

A favorite combination of the Maltese Grill's executive chef, Amey Shaw, of San Francisco.

MAKES 6 SERVINGS

6 to 8 ounces dried wild mushrooms (shiitake, morels, porcini, or Polish)

1½ pounds assorted fresh wild mushrooms (Agarica, chanterelles, oyster, porcini, or shiitake)

Olive oil for sautéeing

3 red onions, sliced

10 garlic cloves, sliced

2 bunches fresh thyme, minced

1 bunch fresh tarragon, minced

Salt and freshly cracked black pepper to taste

12 fresh basil leaves

1 bunch Italian parsley, leaves only

2 bunches curly endive (chicory), cleaned and torn into bite-sized pieces

⅛ cup red wine vinegar

⅛ cup balsamic vinegar

1 cup extra-virgin olive oil

Cover the dried mushrooms with hot water and let stand for 30 minutes. Drain and slice. Clean the fresh mushrooms and slice. In a large sauté pan, over moderately high heat, heat enough olive oil to cover the bottom. When very hot, add the fresh mushrooms and sear; then the rehydrated mushrooms and heat through. Remove the pan from the heat and set aside. Add a little more olive oil to the pan. Sauté the onions until slightly soft. Add the garlic and cook gently until golden, being careful not to burn the garlic. Return the mushrooms to the pan and season with thyme, tarragon, salt, and pepper and remove from heat. Add the basil, parsley, and curly endive to the pan, then both vinegars and the olive oil. Toss and serve immediately.

Hot German Potato Salad with Beer-Braised Sausage

This is a traditional German-style hot potato salad. Use either a waxy red or brown potato, and for an additional treat, caraway seeds.

MAKES 6 TO 8 SERVINGS

6 medium potatoes (about 2½ pounds)

6 slices bacon

½ red onion or 4 shallots, chopped

6 tablespoons white wine vinegar or cider vinegar

¼ cup water

2 tablespoons sugar

1 tablespoon Dijon mustard

1 to 1½ teaspoons salt

¼ teaspoon freshly cracked black pepper

1½ pounds fresh garlic-flavored sausage (see Note)

12 ounces beer

2 tablespoons chopped fresh parsley

Cook the potatoes in boiling salted water to cover until tender, about 30 minutes, drain, and let cool slightly. Peel, dice, and cover with aluminum foil to keep warm.

Dice the bacon and cook over high heat until crisp. Remove with a slotted spoon and drain on paper towels. Add the onion or shallots to the pan and cook until transparent. Stir in the vinegar, water, sugar, mustard, salt, and pepper and bring to a simmer. Taste for seasonings, add the bacon to the pan, and pour over the prepared potatoes. Toss gently to coat.

To cook the sausage, pierce it and place in a skillet with ½ inch of beer. Bring to a simmer, cover, and cook for 20 to 30 minutes. Remove the cover, cook until the juices evaporate and the sausage is brown and crisp. Remove, slice on the diagonal, and arrange around the potato salad. Sprinkle with the chopped parsley. If desired, pour additional ⅓ to ½ cup beer into the pan to deglaze, then reduce slightly. Spoon over sausage.

NOTE: First preference is homemade fresh rabbit or venison sausage, which can be ordered from D'Angelo Brothers Products, Inc., 909 South 9th Street, Philadelphia, PA 19147, 215-923-5637. Bratwurst and knockwurst are good alternatives; they are partially cooked so only steam 10 minutes.

Spinach Waldorf Salad

This is my own variation of a wilted greens salad. The addition of red apples and walnuts makes this a great fall salad.

MAKES 4 SERVINGS

4 ounces fresh spinach

4 slices bacon

1 tablespoon dark brown sugar

1 tablespoon Dijon mustard

4 drops of Tabasco sauce

¼ teaspoon Worcestershire sauce

1½ tablespoons red wine vinegar

5 tablespoons walnut oil

¼ teaspoon salt

⅛ teaspoon freshly cracked black pepper

1 medium red apple

⅓ cup chopped walnuts

Rinse the spinach in several changes of cold water. Drain, remove the stems, and dry leaves. Chill until ready to serve.

Slice the bacon crosswise into ½-inch slices. Cook in a small sauté pan until crisp, remove from the pan with a slotted spoon, and drain on paper towels. Pour off excess fat. In the same pan, blend the brown sugar and mustard. Stir in the next six ingredients and blend well.

Cut the apple into quarters and remove the cores. Slice crosswise into ⅛-inch slices and add to pan. Bring to a simmer and let cook 1 to 2 minutes, stirring occasionally to blend.

Meanwhile, arrange the spinach in a salad bowl and sprinkle with the bacon and walnuts. Pour warm dressing and apples over, toss, and serve.

Pasta with Pesto and Sun-Dried Tomatoes

This salad is a full meal in itself or with the addition of canned drained tuna fish. Pesto can be made in season and refrigerated up to a week, or frozen for future use.

MAKES 6 SERVINGS

1 **pound rotini (twists) pasta**
1½ **cups broccoli florets**
1 **small zucchini, sliced**
1 **small yellow squash, sliced**
½ **red bell pepper, julienne strips**
8 **sun-dried tomatoes in oil, julienne strips**
1¼ to 1½ **cups Pesto Sauce (recipe follows)**
Red or green leaf lettuce
Cherry tomatoes and fresh basil sprigs, for garnish
Pine nuts, for garnish (optional)

Cook the pasta in boiling salted water until al dente, 8 to 10 minutes. Drain and transfer to a bowl. While the pasta is cooking, add the broccoli florets to a small saucepan of boiling water and cook 3 to 4 minutes until tender-crisp. Remove with a slotted spoon and rinse quickly with cold water to set the color and to stop the cooking action. In the same pan, cook the zucchini and yellow squash about 30 seconds until tender-crisp. Drain and rinse quickly to set color. Add the cooked vegetables, red pepper strips, and sun-dried tomatoes to pasta. Toss with enough Pesto Sauce to coat.

Serve on lettuce-lined platter or in a bowl and garnish with cherry tomatoes and fresh basil sprigs. Sprinkle with toasted pine nuts, if desired.

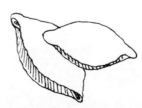

Pesto Sauce

MAKES 1½ CUPS

2½ cups fresh basil leaves
5 tablespoons pine nuts
3 garlic cloves
¼ cup chopped fresh parsley
1 teaspoon salt
¼ to ½ teaspoon freshly cracked black pepper
⅔ cup olive oil
4 tablespoons butter, room temperature
¾ cup Parmesan cheese, cubed or grated

Put all ingredients into a food processor or blender and process until they resemble a coarse purée. Bring to room temperature before using.

Pasta Salad Caldo

If you've been at the pool or at the office all day, this is a great quick-cook supper using fresh summer ingredients. Serve with crusty bread or rolls and a chunk of cheese.

MAKES 4 TO 6 SERVINGS

5 large ripe tomatoes, seeded and cubed
3 garlic cloves, minced
½ cup fresh basil leaves, cut in strips
¾ cup plus 1 tablespoon extra-virgin olive oil
1 cup pitted black olives, halved or quartered lengthwise
1½ pounds fettucine
¼ cup minced fresh parsley
½ cup sautéed or toasted pine nuts
½ cup freshly grated Parmesan cheese
1 to 1½ teaspoons salt
Freshly cracked black pepper, to taste
1 to 2 tablespoons red wine vinegar (optional)
Red or green leaf lettuce
Chopped fresh parsley and toasted pine nuts, for garnish

In a large bowl, combine the tomatoes, garlic, basil leaves, ¾ cup olive oil, and the black olives. Set aside.

Bring a large pot of salted water to a boil along with 1 tablespoon olive oil. Add the fettucine gradually, stirring, return to a full boil and cook until al dente, 7 to 8 minutes (less for fresh). Drain, shaking the colander to remove the excess water, and toss immediately with the reserved tomato mixture. Add the parsley, pine nuts, Parmesan, salt, and pepper. If desired, a tablespoon or two of red wine vinegar can be added to balance the flavors. Serve on a platter or in a bowl lined with red or green leaf lettuce and garnished with additional pine nuts and chopped parsley.

Index

pesto sauce, 119
sorbet, 31
vinaigrette, 83
dressing, 50
Beans: *See* Black bean(s); Green beans;
White beans.
Beef. *See* Ground beef; Steak.
Beet(s)
soup with lime, orange, 19
vichyssoise rouge, 28
Belgian endive, Maryland crabmeat and
asparagus on pink, 71
Bisque
coconut, with Hawaiian prawns, 38
mango cream, 9
scallop, with red caviar, 39
two-colored tomato, with basil sorbet
quenelles, 30-31
Black bean(s)
soup with guacamole, 16-17
white beans, and seared tuna, 63
Blueberry
beurre blanc, sweetbreads on exotic
greens with, 107
mint soup, 7
Bluefish with two sauces, smoked, 46-47
Brochette of lamb salad, grilled, 103
Buffalo steak salad with yogurt sauce, 99

C

Cabbage. *See* Red cabbage.
Caesar salad, steak and, 106
Candied walnuts, 96
Cantaloupe soup, with crème de mint,
orange, 11
Cardamom apple sorbet, 5
Carrot soup, cold curried coconut, 20

Cheese
gratin with mâche and sautéed apples,
polenta, 53
See also: Goat cheese.
Chicken breasts
with citrus sauce, 86-87
grilled, Thai style, 94
stir-fried, with clementines, 90-91
warm chile, with cold salsa cruda, 88-89
Chicken livers
rumaki in red cabbage nests, 92-93
Chile(s)
chicken with cold salsa cruda, warm,
88-89
corn cakes, 69
golden gazpacho with serrano, and bay
scallops, 35
green gazpacho with salsa garnish, 34
roasted tomato salsa, 62
three-pepper
escabeche on spinach spirals, 56
soup, 26-27
Chili vinaigrette, 85
Chilled artichoke soup with lemon, 18
Chilled malanga (yam) soup with
fenugreek essence and garlic
chives, 22-23
Chilled roasted eggplant soup, 24
Coconut
bisque with Hawaiian prawns, 38
carrot soup, cold curried, 20
Cold curried coconut carrot soup, 27
Composed veal salad, 105-106
Coriander, fresh tomato soup with, 33
Corn
cakes, chile, 69
soup with roasted red peppers, curried,
21
Cornmeal
chile corn cakes, 69

apple soup with cardamom apple
    sorbet, curried, 4-5
apricot lime soup, spiced, 6
blueberry mint soup, 7
grapefruit, fig, and mint soup, pink, 8-9
mango cream bisque, 9
melon ball soup, 10
orange cantaloupe soup with crème de
    mint, 8
peachy amaretto soup, 10
plum soup, winter, 13
strawberry rhubarb soup, 12

G

Garlic croutons, 67
Gazpacho
    golden, with serrano peppers and bay
        scallops, 35
    green, with salsa garnish, 34
Glaze, orange and lime, 65
Goat cheese
    on bitter greens, 52
    with two tomatoes, chiffonade, 51
Golden gazpacho with serrano peppers
    and bay scallops, 35
Grapefruit, fig, and mint soup, pink, 8-9
Green beans
    and salsify, lobster salad with, 74-75
    with tomato-chive vinaigrette, curried
        bay scallops and, 76-77
Green gazpacho with salsa garnish, 34
Green pepper(s)
    purée, spicy, 27
    three-pepper
        escabeche on spinach spirals, 56
        soup, 26-27
    See also: Chile(s); Poblano peppers.

Grilled brochette of lamb salad, 103
Grilled chicken, Thai style, 94
Grilled salmon with mixed country greens
    and soy dressing, 57
Grilled sea and forest salad, 84-85
Grilled swordfish with orange and lime
    glaze, 64-65
Ground beef salad olé with plantains,
    100-101
Guacamole, 17, 89

H

Halibut
    three-pepper escabeche on spinach
        spirals, 56
Hearty cucumber soup with smoked
        scallops, 41
Herb
    -garden salad with "paradise" crusted
        scallops, 80-81
    and wild mushroom salad, fresh, 115
Honeydew
    melon ball soup, 10
Horseradish
    cream, 47
    croutons, 77
Hot German potato salad with
        beer-braised sausage, 116

L

Lamb
    Melba, 106
    salad
        grilled brochette of, 103
        with mixed greens, marinated, 102

Plum soup, winter, 13
Poached salad fillets with dill pesto and
wild rice salad, 58-60
Poblano pepper(s)
green gazpacho with salsa garnish, 34
Polenta cheese gratin with mâche and
sautéed apples, 52-53
Potato(es)
leek, and fennel soup, 25
salad, hot German, with beer-braised
sausage, 116
warm scallop, and mâche salad, 78-79
vichyssoise rouge, 28
Prawns, Hawaiian, coconut bisque with,
38

R

Red cabbage
rumaki in, nests, 92-93
salad, 93
Red pepper(s)
vinaigrette, 111
See also: Chile(s).
Rhubarb soup, strawberry, 12
Rice. *See*: Wild rice.
Roasted tomato salsa, 62
Roasted tomato vinaigrette, 47
Rotini
pasta with pesto and sun-dried
tomatoes, 118-119
Rumaki in red cabbage nests, 92-93

S

Salad dressings
bacon onion vinaigrette, 81

balsamic vinaigrette, 51
basil
vinaigrette, 83
dressing, 50
chili vinaigrette, 85
lime vinaigrette, 59
maple vinaigrette, 112
orange vinaigrette, 73
pancetta dressing, four-endive salad
with hot, 114
pesto sauce, 119
red pepper vinaigrette, 111
roasted tomato vinaigrette, 47
soy dressing, 57
tarragon vinaigrette, 97
tomato
-chive vinaigrette, 77
herb vinaigrette, 75
vinaigrette
dressing, 70
Mendoza, 78-79
Salads. *See*: Appetizer(s); Entrée salads;
Side dishes.
Salmon
grilled, with mixed country greens and
soy dressing, 57
poached, fillets with dill pesto and wild
rice salad, 58-60
Salsa
cruda, 89
roasted tomato, 62
Sauce(s)
curry, 75
horseradish cream, 47
pesto, 119
dill, 60
Sausage, beer-braised, hot German potato
salad with, 116
Sautéed crabmeat with chile corn cakes,
68-69

W

Waldorf salad, spinach, 117
Walnuts, candied, 96
Warm chile chicken with cold salsa cruda, 88-89
Warm duck confit with wild mushrooms and seasonal greens, 96-97
Warm lobster salad with fruited pico de gallo, 72-73
Warm scallop, potato, and mâche salad, 78-79
Warm shrimp and artichoke salad with orzo, 82-83
White beans, black beans, and seared tuna, 63
Wild mushroom(s)
fresh herb and, salad, 115
scallop and, salad on greens, 79
and seasonal greens, warm duck confit with, 96-97
Wild rice salad, 59
Wilted Southern greens with apples, pecans, and cranberries, 113
Winter plum soup, 13

Y

Yams
chilled malanga (yam) soup with fenugreek essence and garlic chives, 22-23